Unlocking My Spiritual Self

Library of Congress Cataloguing-in-Publication Data

Silvira, Tony
Unlocking My Spiritual Self, Tony Silvira

ISBN 978-0-9920630-0-9

Self-Help / Inspirational / Spiritual

Dedication

Ana Paula Lopes
October 28, 1963 - August 10, 2008

This Book was written in honour of my wife who bestowed upon me the opportunity to grow in love and awaken to see beyond illusion. This book is dedicated to all those who were part of this journey, including all caregivers, family, and friends.

Table of Contents

Greater love hath no man than this that a man lay down his life for his friends. John 15:13

Forward

Unlocking My Spiritual Self is a book about the cycle of life and death and how there is help for all of us as we walk this path. If you dare to read it, be prepared to be moved.

Unlocking My Spiritual Self is a remarkable book, written by a remarkable man, who is willing to share his journey through heartbreak, illness and death with the intention of encouraging and inspiring others who may have to tread the same path.

Unlocking My Spiritual Self is conveniently divided into two parts. The first part summarizes Tony's journey through cancer with his wife and how it led him to producing his Prayer Wheel Flows.

This is a true story about a journey that none of us wants to have to undertake, being with our partner or loved one as they suffer through life-threatening illness and finally die. It is a journey so painful that most of us try to find ways to escape, seeking out other opinions, other treatments and treatment units to care for our loved ones because it's too painful for us to sit with them.

I first met Tony when he was in the middle of this journey. His wife had been diagnosed with cancer that was expected to be terminal. While mobile she spent much of her time, with Tony's assistance, investigating all sorts of treatment alternatives and following up by meeting many therapists and healers whose methods offered hope. By the time we met, Tony had lost his business, his home and his health as he stood by his wife trying to help her on her journey to healing.

In the final years of his wife's illness she was confined to a bed. There was nothing for Tony to do but sit with her, to be there when she needed something and then wait until he was needed again. To assist him in these sad, solitary and lonely times Tony started using THE PRAYER WHEEL™ Program. He would use it to seek answers to questions he had and he would bring his writings which he called "flows" to our sessions for discussion. It quickly became apparent to Tony, who has never considered himself a writer, that there was something different about his "flows". Not only did they provide answers to his questions, but they appeared to have been much wider, deeper and had a spiritual meaning that seemed to speak to anyone who read them.

Tony used his flows to help his wife and himself through the last steps of her earthly journey. And he shares with us a number of profound, unexplainable and spiritual incidents he experienced before and after his wife's death.

The second part of Unlocking My Spiritual Self contains a sample of more than 40 of the many flows that Tony has collected. Just as the first part is emotionally moving the second part is spiritually moving. The prayer wheel flows are reproduced as originally written without editing, except for spelling corrections and punctuation. There is something here for everyone regardless of background or beliefs. The wisdom, insight and inspiration contained within these flows must be experienced to be understood. Tony does not ask us to take his word, rather he describes the path he has walked, and what he has experienced and how you (the reader) can use the tools he used to help him along his way.

The most profound insight from this book is that help can come to all of us, even in the most difficult circumstances and usually from places most of us never expected.

John F. Rossiter-Thornton, Toronto, August, 2012

MY STORY

It's not easy bearing witness to the suffering of someone else, especially if it's someone whom you love. I have to give my wife credit, even though her fear was apparent to those around her, she had immense courage. Her courage was quiet in nature; the type of courage that can only be appreciated or understood in hindsight. My wife gave everything to cancer, and some may say she lost everything to cancer; including her career, her home, her physical beauty, her ability to walk, and her independence. It always breaks my heart when I think of how much she suffered.

First she put her faith in others; doctors, priests, spiritual healers and alternative medicine. When she saw no improvement in her health she turned inward and began to bargain with god. When she saw no improvement again she tiredly surrendered and became quiet, this was while in palliative care toward the end of her experience with cancer.

My wife fought to stay alive for years for fear of dying. Death was a taboo subject and never a topic of conversation during her 11 years of living with cancer. It was understood that death was a frightening prospect for her and this was quite evident with the many anxiety attacks she had suffered.

I recall one day receiving a phone call at the office, she was in a panic. "Come quickly there's something wrong. I can't stop shaking, please hurry." I could tell in her voice she was scared, so I left immediately and when I arrived, I noticed the front door was left ajar. I pushed open the door and found her shaking uncontrollably on the dining room floor. She told me she had called an ambulance and that's why the door was left open. The ambulance arrived and rushed her to the hospital. Later that night, a doctor came to me to explain the situation. The doctor said that she had suffered an anxiety attack; he also said that her cancer situation was very critical. I told him not to say anything to her and that I would handle it.

My heart was breaking for her as I reassured her that everything was going to be fine. I knew that a decision had to be made that would change both our lives forever. I was scared, but my heart seemed to be stronger and started overpowering my mind. My heart was telling me to close my business because it was the right thing to do and supporting my wife through this very difficult and serious situation was more important than money. However, my mind was in fear and was persuading me to find a way to go forward with the business while still caring for my wife.

I knew how difficult it would be to find a prospective buyer for my business on short notice and I also understood the energy that would be required in dealing with the daily demands and challenges of running a business. With this in mind and coupled with having to support my terrified wife through her fear and cancer treatments left me feeling trapped. I couldn't sleep for two nights while pacing back and forth throughout the night. I don't know why, but my heart won the battle over my mind and I decided to close the business.

I called a lawyer and discussed my situation and his advice was for me to simply walk away from my business. I was somewhat perplexed and I asked him what he meant by "walk away." He told me that I needed to look after my wife because she was dying, and since I was incorporated I should just walk away from the business. I became concerned when he told me that there would be people that would not be pleased with this decision and he told me that I should disappear for a while. The lawyer further stated that some people are only concerned about money and couldn't care less about personal circumstances, and since I was walking away from my business, the landlord would take over all of my assets. This meant that all my suppliers would have to deal directly with the landlord and some would end up taking more, while others would end up losing more and would not be happy. The lawyer advised me that this should be the least of my worries as I was about to lose everything and my suppliers have insurance.

It was time to let my wife know of my decision. When I told her, she immediately went into a panic; she asked me, “How are we going to survive?” “Where are we going to live?” “What about my cancer, we need money for my treatments?” “What are people going to think?” “What are people going to do to us?” She told me that if we had to disappear for a while, that meant our poor parents were going to be harassed and it would not be fair to put them through that. I understood her fears because I too had asked myself those same questions. I wished there was another way, but there wasn't. I had no choice but to reassure my wife that everything would work out in the end and that her health was the only priority now and that nothing else mattered.

Going forward was difficult, more difficult than I could have possibly imagined. We went into hiding and were living out of a small room. There were rumours circulating that we took off with hundreds of thousands of dollars and fled to Brazil and people were looking to physically harm me. Our mail was being stolen from our house which was now up for sale. Someone had placed a garden hose in one of the lower case windows and flooded the basement. One day we walked into our house to find that someone had tampered with the gas and the temperature inside was hovering around 35 degrees Fahrenheit, and if that were not enough, my wife had been given a year to live.

I woke up every morning with my body shaking uncontrollably. I experienced shortness of breath; it felt like an elephant was sitting on my chest. I sensed a need to get up, move, and wash my face to try and control my thoughts. I was clearly overwhelmed and I was struggling with my circumstances as my wife looked toward me for strength. I felt an obligation and a duty to be strong for her, but yet, I was exhausted with the amount of challenges I had to face daily; I wondered how I would manage to get through each day.

I realized that I had to accept the reality of my situation. I had to surrender to this reality, "It is what it is." Mind over matter was no longer working for me; it was not enough anymore and was weakening as I found myself humbled by my circumstances. I found myself unable to be strong mentally without the assistance of my heart. I was forced to surrender and let go to the way of my ego. I sensed a change within me as this experience was now beginning to break down my personality. This was the first true awakening I had to the strength within my heart; to the possibility that my heart may be stronger and wiser than my mind. The question that still remained unanswered was, am I falling apart or am I getting stronger?

With all the stressful events that shadowed our every move, I decided it was time to shelter my wife from all the bad news so that she could focus solely on her healing. The only conversations allowed between us were healing related and staying hopeful was our priority. Focusing on attitude, proper diet, supplements, exercise, and living one day at a time took center stage, while all the other bad stuff happening to us was secondary and was my responsibility.

A year had passed and my wife was holding up well, it seemed that we were finally on top of this cancer thing. This of course was very good news for us, and yet, I sensed that some of those close to us were beginning to wonder if there was any truth to some of the rumours that were circulating. I heard comments like, "For someone who was given a year to live she looks pretty good." Or "You can't tell by looking at her that she has cancer." It wasn't so much what was said that bothered me, but how it was said that made me uncomfortable. A part of me wanted to be defensive, but what would be the point; I knew the truth, and right now that was all that mattered.

It was comforting to know that I was not a criminal, a con artist, or a lying cheat. This knowledge about myself allowed me to face my life circumstances with a sense of dignity. I thought that with time the rumour mill would subside, but unfortunately, that would not be the case. Gossip, especially negative gossip is like food for many. There must be a reason why people take pleasure in hearing about another's so called fall from grace. As a result of this life experience I learned not to judge others so quickly. I believe this speaks to why truth cannot be found within judgement.

We all have to exit this world one day. The question is, how are we going to exit and when are we going to exit? This is not something that we think about on a daily basis. Imagine having to live knowing how and approximately when you are going to die. Imagine having to face this reality every day and having to get up every morning with this reality; it can't be easy. In retrospect, I realized that I didn't give my wife enough credit. Even though she feared death, she got up every morning and dealt with it and that takes courage.

The "natural" approach seemed to be working for us, so we continued to explore this avenue further. Twice a month, we drove two and a half hours north of Toronto to see Dr. Sat Dharam Kaur.

Dr. Kaur is a naturopathic doctor practicing in Owen Sound, Ontario at Grey-Bruce Naturopathic Centre. Dr. Kaur believes that the better we understand the origins of this disease, the better our ability to prevent it. Dr. Kaur developed the "Healthy Breast Program" to provide a naturopathic protocol for preventing and treating breast cancer to be used in combination with allopathic diagnostic and treatment options. Besides being an expert in this field, she is also a compassionate, caring, and gentle soul. There was something about her angelic voice that always seemed to give my wife hope.

Everything was going fine, or so it seemed until the day my wife felt a slight lump on her other breast. At the next meeting with her oncologist she mentioned the lump and he immediately set up an appointment to have a biopsy.

A week or so had passed since the biopsy and we were on our way to the hospital to see the oncologist for the results. It was a warm summer day and we were driving with the windows rolled down. We approached a busy intersection in downtown Toronto and there was a lot of noise around us. The sound of car horns, cars accelerating, people talking, and trucks and streetcars moving, our car radio was playing, but not too loud, when all of a sudden everything fell silent. It was the strangest feeling, the background noise around me seemed to vanish and all I could hear was a male voice in the distance speaking to a group of people. They were standing off to my right approximately 30 feet away from our car. I could hear his voice and nothing else. This male voice entered the car as clear as if he were sitting next to me and all I heard was, "Stay the Course." I remember thinking to myself that this was weird! I turned to my wife and asked, "Did you hear that?" By her expression, I already knew what her response would be. With all the noise around us she'd reply with, "Hear what?" This was exactly what she said.

We arrived at Women's College Hospital, it was late afternoon and I was feeling somewhat anxious, I could only imagine how my wife was feeling. She was quiet and deep in thought as I reached for her hand and held it firmly. She let out a gentle sigh as she turned her head toward me. My wife looked into my eyes with a look of deep dejection; I smiled and nodded my head slightly to convey that things would be okay. I was asking myself what will be next, what will I do or say if we get bad news. I wondered how or if the news would change what we've been doing and if this would cause her to lose hope.

We had been waiting for over an hour, the waiting room was now empty and we were the only ones left in the room. My wife turned to me and said, “I already know it's not going to be good news.” I looked into her eyes and asked her why she would say that. My wife responded by saying, “Because we are the last appointment, and like all the other times before, they need to spend more time with me when it's bad news.” Sadly, this made perfect sense to me, but I still felt the need to respond with something positive to let her know that everything would be fine no matter what. So, I responded by telling her that no matter what the news was we would just “stay the course.” I couldn't believe what just came out of my mouth, “Stay the Course.” Those were the same words I heard spoken earlier that day at the busy intersection; now that strange experience just became more meaningful to me.

Our oncologist entered the room with his usual warm smile and said, “Sorry to keep you waiting, come on in.” Suddenly, for some unexplained reason I had an uncomfortable feeling throughout my body and sensed that something was wrong. You can call it a hunch or a gut feeling, it doesn't matter, it was real. We both sat directly in front of his desk while looking for any negative signs; the tone in his voice, his eye contact, his posture, his demeanor, anything at all. Five minutes or so had passed and we had our answer; we knew that it was not good. If it were to be good news, then the doctor would have made it known to us within the first minutes. Instead, the doctor began by giving us statistics and related data. A sinking feeling began to envelop me as I looked toward my wife knowing that she was feeling what I was feeling. Now we were in no hurry to hear the news that we so feared. The news could wait and we just allowed the doctor to continue with his long and deliberate presentation intended to soften the blow.

Once again, we left the hospital with a feeling of despair and sadness. My wife began to cry when she entered the car. I was silent as I watched the tears run down her cheeks and I too wanted to cry. It hurt me so much to see my wife's fear, pain and anguish; I wished that I could take it all away. Through her tears, I saw the vulnerability of a child who was lost and afraid and wanting someone to make this all go away. She turned toward me and asked what she did that was so bad to deserve so much suffering. In a meek voice she said, “I'm not a bad person and I don't hurt others. Why is god doing this to me, why? I was at a loss for words and all I could do was to listen with sadness. Then, what seemed like out of nowhere that phrase came to me, “Stay the Course." It kept repeating itself in my head, “Stay the Course, Stay the Course, Stay the Course.” I sensed a real power and wisdom within those words that I had to speak them out loud to her. I looked into my wife's eyes and with a confident voice told her that this was far from over and we were going to stay the course. I told her that it was one day at a time and that we needed to stay the course. I told her that we didn't know what the outcome would be, but we must stay the course. I knew that we couldn't give up and that we had to believe while staying the course! In time, I could see that this was beginning to have a positive effect and my wife's tears slowly began to dry. A sense of calm seemed to envelope her as she began to regain control over her circumstance, even if only temporary.

An appointment was made the next day to see Dr. Kaur. We made the usual two and a half hour drive to Owen Sound. We both needed answers as we had many questions. We questioned the following: If my wife was eating organically, taking her supplements religiously, walking 5-7 kilometers a day and taking all the necessary steps to reduce the stress associated with cancer, then why did a lump now appear in the other breast. Why was this cancer progressing and not regressing with all that we were doing?

We arrived and as always were greeted with a warm and loving hug from Dr. Kaur. My wife began to explain her new situation and in the process began to cry. Dr. Kaur had been a counselor as well as a naturopathic doctor to my wife since they met. My wife had not seen anyone professionally to deal with her anxieties since she was first diagnosed with cancer. Dr. Kaur had been a grief counselor, psychologist and psychiatrist to her, but her recommendation was for my wife to find someone closer to her in Toronto to help her with her anxiety and fear; a professional who specialized in dealing with people living with cancer.

All my wife wanted and needed was to feel hopeful, she wanted to be reassured that she was on the right path toward healing. My wife desperately needed to hear that she could and would beat cancer. Dr. Kaur, through her gentleness and compassion had always been able to reassure and offer hope, but realized that my wife also needed someone closer to her to see her on a regular basis.

Dr. Kaur suggested that we contact Well Spring in Toronto. Well Spring is a network of cancer support centers providing programs, educational resources and training for cancer patients and their families. We were given the name of a grief counselor who volunteered her services there a couple of times a week. It seemed that anxiety, anger, and fear were negating factors and counterproductive to healing. Emotional healing and a positive attitude are essential to healing your body from cancer, and this was something that had been ignored thus far. This made a lot of sense to my wife and she was determined to make changes. We headed back home with a renewed sense of optimism and confidence.

That same evening my wife was watching a television program called "Health on Line" and the topic was healing yourself using the power of intention. They were interviewing a young boy named Adam. Adam is a gifted young energy healer who reveals the interconnectedness of energy systems in order to prepare people to embrace their own healing power. My wife called me with excitement, "Hurry, come quickly, you need to see this!" It was rare to hear enthusiasm in her voice, so I hurried to see what all the fuss was about. At the end of the program, my wife asked me to look Adam up on the internet. I found that he was doing a workshop the following week in Toronto. My wife was ecstatic and told me that she had to meet with him.

The workshop was sold out, but this was not enough to deter my wife; she was determined to meet Adam. She noticed that 10% of the proceeds would be going to Gilda's Club in Toronto. Gilda's Club is a cancer support organization. My wife called them and explained her situation and as a result, Gilda's Club gave my wife the only ticket they had left free of charge. Gilda's Club staff then called Adam's father to advise him of our circumstances, and as a result, Adam's father allowed me to accompany my wife as a guest.

The following week, we attended the workshop. We arrived early because my wife wanted to make sure that we would get a front row seat. Adam's topic was so foreign to me and I was very skeptical. I didn't want to spoil this event for my wife, but I also would not allow her to be given false hope as some part of a scam. A part of me wanted to believe that gifted people truly existed and another part of me was looking for the proverbial money angle. I had to be smart and use my business sense in the event that this turned out to be just another "snake oil salesman."

The workshop began with Adam's father introducing his son. The father appeared to be genuine, but I refused to be swayed by this and remained on guard. Adam entered to a big applause, he looked to be very young, a teenager about sixteen years old. I did not expect someone so young to be speaking on such a serious topic. My skepticism caused me to question whether a father would use his teenage son to con people, especially vulnerable sick people who were suffering with cancer.

Adam spoke for approximately 5 hours without using notes. I was struck by the nature of his presentation which appeared to be far beyond his years. He was very articulate, poised, and confident and seemed to be very knowledgeable, yet, I still questioned the authenticity of this young boy. At one point during the presentation, Adam's father reminded the audience that there was nothing wrong with skepticism as long as an open mind was maintained. He went on to say that in the beginning, he too was skeptical of his son's abilities; especially since he came from a scientific background. Again, I found myself wondering if this was part of the scam in order to gain our trust.

At the end of the workshop there was a book signing. The line-up was long and we decided to wait until the end as this would give us more time to speak with Adam. As we approached his table, I realized that I was about to speak to a kid regarding a serious health matter. This sounded crazy to me, and yet, Adam seemed very genuine. His youthful innocence and polite, unpretentious demeanor got my attention. He was not trying to sell anything, not even his $10 book which he wrote to help people understand their true potential to heal. Being a skeptic, I was always looking for the money angle so this appeared rather odd to me. I witnessed many desperate people seeking help from Adam and his father. Many of these people wanted to have a personal consultation with Adam and were willing to pay a lot of money for this. To my surprise, Adam and his father refused to take money from these people. As a result, my money angle theory was slowly fading, but I remained guarded.

In his presentation, Adam mentioned that worry was a waste of time and energy; a positive expectation is essential to healing. I realized that this tied into Dr. Kaur's theory and this had us both thinking that we were on the right path toward healing. Recognizing the importance emotions play in healing, my wife decided that it was time to call Wellspring.

An appointment was made to see Dr. Vachon, one of the volunteers there. Dr. Vachon is a grief counsellor as well as a psychologist; if there is anyone who understands the cancer journey, it's Dr. Vachon. Dr. Vachon herself battled a rare form of cancer and today she is cancer free.

We met with Dr. Vachon through Wellspring on three separate occasions. Since Wellspring only allows for three free consultations, Dr. Vachon offered to see us through her private practice. My wife was finally talking to someone about her feelings; she opened up about her childhood memories, fears and her anxieties. This process was very difficult for her considering she was a very private person. Dr. Vachon suggested a book written by Wayne Dyer called, "The Power of Intention." We couldn't help but think of the correlation between the title of the book and Adam's recent presentation on using intention to heal. This piqued our curiosity even further and had us questioning and speculating about its significance.

We attempted to read The Power of Intention with great difficulty; we had never read anything that was spiritual in nature before. Many of the terms and phrases were completely foreign to us. We had to read and reread each sentence at least a dozen times, and still, we found it difficult to make sense of what was being said. I remember asking Dr. Vachon, “Do people really speak this way?” If it were not for the synchronicity of these events, we probably would have stopped reading this book. We believed that there must have been a reason why two identical and unrelated events entered our lives at this particular time. We continued to open ourselves up more to “thinking outside of the box."

Dr. Vachon believed that I too could benefit from counselling, she asked me if I would be comfortable talking to someone who would be open to these types of things. Dr. Vachon was referring to a doctor who was spiritual in nature; someone who was unconventional in their approach to psychotherapy.

I agreed and an appointment was made to see this doctor, his name was Dr. John Thornton. Dr. Thornton is a psychiatrist who co-founded the Spirituality In Health Care Network in December of 2000 in Toronto. The Spirituality in Health Care Network (SHCN) is a network of professionals and spiritual leaders dedicated to integrating Spirituality with Psychotherapy and Health Care. Dr. Thornton also created “The Prayer Wheel Program,” which is a secular, non-denominational way to pray. It shows people how to use the ancient power of prayer without the dogma, because it was designed initially for use in clinical practice. This was my first time seeing a psychiatrist, and for some reason I regarded this as a sign of weakness. I felt the self-conscious emotions of shame, pride, and embarrassment. I held the stereotypical view that one had to be "crazy" in order to see a psychiatrist. In order to make myself feel more at ease, I told myself that no one would know that I was here today with the exception of my wife and she would not tell anyone. I thought that if anything, it may better help me to cope with my situation; I didn't know what to expect, but I felt that I needed to take this step.

While I was sitting in the waiting room of Dr. Thornton's office, the door opened and I was offered to take a seat. My eyes were immediately drawn to the “notorious” couch. I told myself that there was no way I was going to lay down on that couch. I chose to take a seat on the couch and position myself directly across from him. Everything appeared to be going well, I felt comfortable, and the conversation and questioning seemed what I would consider typical. Then, Dr. Thornton blind-sided me with what I regarded as an aggressive, confrontational statement. He said, "What if I were to tell you that you created all of this yourself, and what if I were to tell you that you are responsible for all of this." I felt like he was pressuring me, attacking me, and blaming me; I didn't like it at all and I became angry wondering what was going on. I responded with, "You think I wanted this to happen to me, and are you saying that this is my fault?" After, what seemed like an eternity, the appointment came to an end and I left feeling frustrated, angry, and confused.

The following week, my wife and I met with Dr. Vachon for her weekly consultation. The consultation was approaching the end when Dr. Vachon asked me how my session went with Dr. Thornton. I proceeded to tell her how he attacked me and made me feel as though I was responsible for everything. I also told her that I would never go back to him. Dr. Vachon seemed very surprised and somewhat shocked by this and told me that she would have a word with him.

My wife and I met again the following week with Dr. Vachon and she tried to convince me to see Dr. Thornton one more time. I told her once again that I would never go back and Dr. Vachon told me that she spoke with Dr. Thornton and told him to "BACK OFF" and that things would be different this time. After giving it some thought, I decided to take her advice and give it another try. I found myself back in the waiting room nervously waiting to see Dr. Thornton when an elderly lady exited his office; she looked right at me and said, "He's a bad man!" Needless to say, I began preparing myself to bolt out of the office when all of a sudden I heard his voice telling me to come in. I entered his office with trepidation and to my surprise the meeting went rather smoothly this time. At the end of the session I left feeling better about my decision to see him again.

Whether it was an accident, luck, or fate, the coincidences kept appearing; my wife had what she termed a "healing dream." In her dream, she was staring into the sun; she described it as a bright yellow ball. Later that same day we were in the car headed to the lake for our daily walk and we stopped to pick up a juice smoothie.

The car was parked by a newspaper box and for some reason my wife was drawn to it. She got out of the car and opened the box pulling out a booklet from the Learning Annex and noticed an advertisement. Within this advertisement, there was a picture of an Asian man in a suit and beside him; there was a picture of a golden shining ball which looked like the sun. He was to be giving a presentation on Soul Mind Body Space Medicine at a convention center in Toronto. My wife thought that this could be a sign, and with all the unexplained coincidences lately she was eager to attend.

My wife and I were of the opinion that the book by Wayne Dyer on intention and our meeting Adam had awakened us to thinking outside of the box. Little did we know that this would only serve as a warm up to what we were about to witness and experience from the Asian man in the suit.

His name is Dr. Sha also known as Master Zhi Gang Sha. Dr. Sha was trained as a Western medical doctor, but is also a doctor of traditional Chinese medicine. He is considered an expert in advanced cellular healing, a science being developed in China, and is also involved in Western research on the effects of the spirit on the body. He is also the founder of the Institute of Soul Healing and Enlightenment and the World Soul Healing, Peace and Enlightenment Movement. Dr. Sha's lineage can be traced 5,000 years and includes Buddhist and Taoist secrets. He is a grandmaster of numerous ancient orders including Feng Shui and Tai Chi.

We attended his seminar and were being shown for the first time the concept of Karma and its relationship to illness. Karma is past life mistakes which impact our present lives. We heard about his spiritual journey and how his third eye opened. Third eye is the ability to see, hear, and communicate with the spiritual world. We heard about his direct communication with god, akashic records, spiritual debt, soul over matter, soul language, soul operation, golden healing ball, and transmissions or spiritual downloads. This all seemed so foreign, crazy, and yet plausible.

During the first break we found ourselves looking around at all the people in the room wondering if they were sane or insane. We wondered if people actually believed in this. We decided to talk to a few of the people and we soon realized that these were educated and intelligent people who appeared to understand our skepticism. With this in mind, we agreed to stay until the end of Dr. Sha's presentation.

Master Sha gave a spiritual blessing to everyone present, and then asked if anyone saw anything with their third eye. To our surprise a few people raised their hands in the air to share their third eye experiences. As these individuals shared their experiences, we wondered if they were genuine or a part of a scam. This was so foreign to us that we had to talk to some of those same people during the next break in order to put our suspicions to rest. We cornered a few people during the break and were once again surprised at their ability to come across in a very genuine manner.

Toward the end of the evening, Master Sha's assistant addressed the audience. We were told that Master Sha would be performing a Karma cleansing for all those interested. There was so much emphasis that evening put on the importance of Karma and how it affects our present life's challenges. We were told that Master Sha is one of the only few people in the world with the spiritual ability to clear karma. Apparently, karma is a debt owed for past mistakes for harming others, and this creates our present life lessons. This includes financial, spiritual, marital, and illness related lessons.

Call us crazy, but we were sold! Here is what happened; we both stood side by side next to Master Sha's table. Master Sha appointed a third eye reader to describe to us what they saw at the end of the karma cleansing. We were told to close our eyes and to stand still with our arms by our side. Then, Master Sha told us to thank Divine for this great blessing. In a stern loud voice he said BEGIN! Within a few seconds, a tremendous surge of energy was felt throughout my entire body. It felt as if my body was out of control and my arms were flailing, I wanted to open my eyes to see if this was the case; I wanted to control myself for fear of looking silly. Something told me to just go with the flow and let it happen. The energy surge came to an end after what felt like a minute or two; I was somewhat speechless when it was over. I was thinking to myself that something definitely happened and that I was not dreaming, but I didn't have an explanation to make sense of this experience. The third eye reader began to describe what she saw and it was not very flattering.

According to the third eye reader, my book of life or akashic record was stained and full of wrong doings which she went on to describe. After the karma cleansing, the pages of my book of life were now clear and no longer stained according to the third eye reader. I know if someone were to tell me something like this, I would be very skeptical and would question their sanity. The fact is that something, although unclear, happened to my body and I know that what I experienced was real.

My wife befriended one of Master Sha's assistants. This woman was bright, articulate, sophisticated, business minded, and deeply spiritual. She also had her third eye open and was able to access akashic records. I asked this woman why I was having such a difficult time accepting Master Sha. She told me that it was because I tend to think from the "neck up." I wondered what she meant by that. She went on to explain that I don't think from the neck down with my heart. She said she understood this was not something that the logical mind alone would understand. The fact is, if this woman did not demonstrate astuteness in my presence, I would have had a much easier time discrediting her. She was an executive in the business world, an image consultant, and at one time married to a court judge. Now she wanted to introduce my wife and I to another gifted person who goes by the name of Brian Farnum. He is known as the "Truth Oracle." He is able to access truth on a yes and no basis. I found myself asking yet again, was I going crazy or are these people around us crazy?

It was a Friday evening and we were on our way to hear Brian Farnum speak for the first time. His lecture was being held at a banquet hall at a golf course in Markham, Ontario. We were seated awaiting his entrance and we looked around curiously at the others, wondering if they were sane like us or if they were also questioning our sanity for being here tonight! There was an empty aisle running down the middle of the room which divided the seating area. I did a head count to pass time and there was approximately forty people in the room.

It was now 7:00 pm and Brian entered from the back of the room. He was an opposing figure; he stood about six feet five inches tall. As he began to speak, I quickly realized that he was a gentle soul. He spoke in a manner that was completely different from Master Sha, and yet, I could see parallels and similarities in his message. He spoke in a very direct manner; he challenged you to become aware of your sense of responsibility to your life circumstances. He spoke about past lives and the power of forgiveness and he spoke of how thoughts create illness. His approach was blunt and he would say what needed to be said. Brian explained how truth often hurts, but that the truth is the truth and people need to face the truth of their lives in order to heal. Brian stated that common sense originates in the heart and not the mind. He further stated that one feels truth in the heart and that is why he speaks directly to one's heart. I have to say that I did feel a sense of truth in his words; it was a very interesting evening for sure.

During my weekly sessions with Dr. Thornton, I found myself repeatedly picking his brain in an attempt to convince myself of Adam, Dr. Sha, and Brian Farnum. To my surprise, Dr. Thornton appeared to have no problem accepting their spiritual abilities or philosophies. I would not have expected this from a psychiatrist; this intrigued me and definitely got my attention. I began to contemplate and consider the following: Dr. Thornton is an intellectual; he is well read and has attained a higher education than most people. On the other hand, I didn't have a post-secondary education, and yet, I was the one having difficulty accepting all of this. I thought my psychiatrist would see through this spiritual nonsense, but maybe, I needed to be more open to thinking outside of the box. Perhaps, I needed to realize that there is more to life than meets the eye. Over a period of time and as a result of numerous discussions with Dr. Thornton, I was able to open up to, and accept spirituality as a part of my life. This would prove to be an invaluable tool as my journey into the unfamiliar continued.

One morning in the middle of the night I awakened to a loud voice in my head. This was not a thought that entered my mind and this was not a dream either. This voice was not mine; it was masculine and the tone very assertive. The voice said: "WAKE…… UPPPPPPPPPPPPPP." I woke up all right; I sprang up, eyes wide open, with the last word of the voice "UP" still ringing in my ears for approximately thirty seconds. The ringing in my ears was so loud that it unquestionably got my attention; I didn't know what this meant. I thought it had something to do with my wife being in pain, and that I had to wake up to help her. This would explain it, so I thought, except for the fact that she was comfortably asleep. What was haunting to me about this experience was the fact that I heard a foreign voice within me for a noticeable period of time as I sat fully awake. I brought this up at my next session with Dr. Thornton and to my surprise he didn't think I was losing my mind. In fact, he thought this was real and that I needed to question its significance.

My wife and I continued to do everything we could to overcome and defeat her cancer. We attended a lecture given by Charlotte Gerson on The Gerson Therapy. The Gerson Therapy seeks to regenerate the body to health, supporting each important metabolic requirement by flooding the body with nutrients from almost 20 pounds of organically grown fruits and vegetables daily. Most is used to make fresh raw juice, one glass every hour, 13 times per day. Dr. Gerson's research indicates that cancer patients must have a two- stage juicer with a separate grinder and hydraulic press. Fortunately, we had a friend who had one and was not using it. We decided to take advantage of this opportunity and incorporate a moderated version of the Gerson Therapy.

My wife was using energy healing, spiritual healing, macro biotic diet, exercise, the Gerson Therapy, positive thinking, and supplementation. With all of this, the cancer continued to spread further into her bones. My wife was now finding it more and more difficult to walk, and morphine had now become part of her daily treatment. My wife couldn't understand why nothing was helping; especially when she was doing so much more than most people she had met. My wife, in frustration said, "Why does it seem that others are having success while I keep getting worse?" It's interesting that all the people we had met told her that she could heal herself following their protocol. Well in fact, my wife was following all their protocols at the same time and logically one would think that by having all her bases covered, she would have seen some encouraging results by now. Instead, my wife continued to get worse and the reason according to some people that we had met was that it was emotional based. Fear of dying seemed to be a big reason, followed by anger on a soul level and not being able to forgive on a heart level. This was so frustrating for my wife because she felt that she was doing the best she could do to address those areas of her life.

The nights were long; we usually got to bed around three in the morning. The pain in her bones kept her up at night; she refused to take more morphine than she had to. We were thinking about hypnosis and how that may help her better cope with her situation when all of a sudden, tragedy struck. If we thought things couldn't get much worse, we were so wrong.

It was my mother- in- law's birthday and we were on our way to visit with her. We arrived at her house, I parked the car and my wife couldn't move; she was unable to move her legs. My wife thought that if she took a breakthrough morphine pill it would allow her to move her legs again. We waited a few minutes for the effects of the morphine to start working, but nothing changed. Fifteen minutes or so went by and my wife still couldn't move her legs. My wife always tried to shelter her family from dealing with her cancer, but this time she had no choice; I had to call her brother from inside the house to come out and help me carry her inside. We carefully picked her up and took her inside and gently placed her in her childhood bedroom on top of her bed. There was a somber atmosphere in the house now, and no one was in the mood to celebrate a birthday under these circumstances.

We spent the night there in the hope that this would pass and that my wife would be able to leave in the morning. This unfortunately did not happen, and one day led to another, then another, and before we knew it a week had passed. The reality that something very serious had happened became very apparent as I sat her up in the bed to wash her; I happened to run my hands down her spine and noticed that it had collapsed. My wife's spine had bowed outward and she was unable to straighten herself up. My wife was not aware of what was causing this, and for fear of her reaction I decided to say nothing at this time.

My wife was now paralyzed and the future was looking bleak. She refused to go to the hospital because, as she put it, “If I go to the hospital, I know I will never come out." In a show of solidarity, I spent my days and nights sitting and sleeping on the floor next to her. I thought to myself that if she had to live in a room, then so would I; we would go through this together and I would not allow her to experience this alone. I spent my days and nights in that room watching her slowly get worse. I began to notice that when she was sleeping, her breathing was becoming laboured. I also began to notice that she was starting to lose weight and her complexion was looking less pinkish and greyer in colour.

Nine months had now passed and we were still living in a room with no view. Winter, spring, and summer had come and gone. My wife’s legs were beginning to swell and I needed to do something. I called my wife's family doctor and she strongly suggested that I get her into a hospital as soon as possible. Knowing that this would be a terrifying prospect for my wife, I knew I had to approach this situation with great care and sensitivity. It took me a few days of gentle persuasion and finally I got my wife to agree. It was very emotional for my wife having to leave her childhood bedroom. I watched her taste fresh air for the first time in over nine months. The expression on my wife's face told me that this was a surreal and dreamlike experience for her. It was extremely heartbreaking for me to watch her expression change to fear as we were nearing the hospital.

We arrived in Emergency and soon after my wife was admitted. She was placed in a shared room where the beds were separated by only a thin curtain. I had to admit that it was nice to be out of her bedroom, but sharing a room in a hospital was not a pleasant change by any means.

Our first roommate was very sick; she had throat cancer and would wander around the room. I offered to watch over her since I would be sleeping in the room by my wife’s side. I was given a chair that reclined to form a bed. It wasn't the most comfortable chair as it was very hard, but by now I had become accustomed to living in these types of conditions. It was very noisy in our room with all the equipment running and hearing the roommates who were also suffering in pain. I eventually bought earplugs so that I could better sleep through the nights.

Eventually, our first roommate was moved to a private room due to her declining health and violent outbursts. The next roommate we received also had advanced cancer. She could not speak and only whispered. I offered to help her as well, and she kept me busy because she was always trying to leave the room during the night. Nurses were nowhere to be found, there never seemed to be enough nurses during the night shift. The following day, this women's daughter came to visit her mother and was told about my having looked after her mother that night. She was very grateful and thanked me as she left the room to allow her mother to rest.

A few hours had passed and the daughter returned and was unable to wake her mother. Frantically, she called the nurse; the nurse arrived and noticed that her mother had passed away. The daughter became distraught and there was a lot of commotion in the room. This situation hit very close to home for my wife and she had an anxiety attack as a result. I attempted to get my wife out of the room in an attempt to calm her, but for some unexplained reason, she refused to leave. Even the nurses were unsuccessful in trying to remove my wife from the room.

This situation was surreal to me as I watched family members arrive with the hospital Chaplain. This was the first time I witnessed death in my presence. To my surprise and amazement I wasn't nervous or scared. I watched the Chaplain and family members encircle the bed to pray the Our Father. When they finished praying, the Chaplain offered his condolences to the family and left the room. I noticed that the family members were still not at ease and did not appear to be comforted, even after having the Chaplain there to offer prayer; this didn't seem right to me. For some unexplained reason I felt compelled to approach this family and offer my condolences, I didn't stop there; something within me wanted to ease their pain. I said a few kind words about their mother and then I told them that their mother was still alive. There was silence and a look of confusion on their faces. I further elaborated on my comment and then went back to sit by my wife's side. There was an uncomfortable silence in the room as I sat next to my wife. The dividing curtain in the room was drawn so the grieving family could not see my wife whisper to me the following, "Why did you go to them and say that, they probably think you're crazy." The longer I sat there thinking about what my wife just said, I began to feel as though I did something wrong and left the room to ponder this.

I went across the hall to the quiet room and sat there hoping that the family would leave before I went back to the room. Instead, the door opened and it was the family coming into the quiet room and I immediately got up to give them privacy. As I made my way toward the door to leave, the daughter stopped me and asked me why I had come over to speak to them. I told her that I felt their pain and thought that the Chaplain did nothing to ease that pain. She then said to me that I had no idea how much they needed to hear that, and she then thanked me from the bottom of her heart. At that moment I felt so relieved and I went back to the room and said to my wife, "So, you think I made a fool of myself, well, that family just thanked me in the quiet room." My wife looked at me with a surprised expression on her face.

Many roommates came and went; almost one every second or third day. This was very challenging as most of these people were seriously ill. I felt a certain amount of empathy which compelled me to reach out to them. Some of the nurses became aware of this and therefore affectionately nicknamed me, "the angel on the sixth floor." By the sixth week, there was a lot of pressure for the hospital to move my wife out and into a palliative unit. They considered my wife to be in a palliative state, but we refused to go. The only other option for us was to go home which was out of the question according to the hospital's palliative doctors. After much discussion, we ended up being moved to a nursing home and placed in a convalescent unit.

The policy of the nursing home only allows people to stay in a convalescent unit for a maximum of three months. This was a better option for my wife's emotional well-being which she could better handle than being placed in a palliative unit at this time. This gave her hope and I would rather see her go through this with hope than with fear; the emotional well-being of my wife was my main priority at this time. Accepting a terminal cancer patient into the nursing home presented a challenge for the staff. The resident doctor made his rounds weekly and he couldn't believe that someone in my wife's condition would be accepted into a convalescent unit, not to mention a nursing home. He told me that a nursing home was not equipped to handle a situation of terminal cancer, especially in my wife's circumstances. I could see his point, but the fact that I was there by my wife's side every day made it easier for the staff. When you page a nurse in ICU, the usual response time is within minutes, but when you page a nurse in a nursing home, the response time is usually within a half hour. By my being there, I was able to advocate and influence the nurses to act out of compassion in order to attend to the needs of my wife in a timely manner.

The three month deadline was fast approaching and my wife was beginning to feel anxious; she knew that she would have to leave the nursing home and didn't want to be placed into a palliative unit. To my wife, this would mean that she was dying and death was something she deeply feared. Having hope helped her cope with her situation by giving her a sense of peace; I was not about to let anyone take that away from her. The only other option was to take her home and this was out of the question due to the fragile state of her bones. What my wife needed more than anything was to be in a supportive environment with doctors and nurses in order for her to feel secure. The only place was for her to go back to the original hospital that we came from. My wife knew that this would be next to impossible and as a result she had a panic attack.

As it turned out, her panic attack got her admitted into the same hospital that we came from. This was due to the responding paramedic's compassion for my wife's situation. The EMS respondents asked their supervisor if they could transport my wife to the hospital of her choice. This meant not following protocol, which requires paramedics to transport all patients to the closest available hospital.

Now back in the same hospital that we originally came from, we were admitted into emergency and were waiting to be seen by the on call oncologist. The oncologist arrived and asked me to leave the room. Normally, I wouldn't leave the room under any circumstance as I have always tried to protect and shield my wife from inappropriate comments that may have a negative impact on her emotional well-being; this time I did leave the room. After a few minutes, the oncologist approached me and told me that my wife was very sick and that she shouldn't be alive. He then said that they would do their best to keep her comfortable and walked away.

I went back to my wife's bedside and with just one look at her face, I knew something wasn't right. I then asked her if she was okay and she responded with, "Do you know what the doctor said to me?" With fear in her eyes she said that the doctor told her that what she had would kill her. I was furious and couldn't believe how irresponsible and cold hearted this doctor was to her. I was so angry that I needed to calm myself down in order not to make a scene that would cause more distress to my wife.

I went in search of the doctor and spotted him talking to a few of his colleagues. I couldn't help myself and interrupted them. I told him that I needed to speak with him and I voiced my disapproval. I asked him why he felt the need to tell my wife that what she had would kill her. He replied by stating that it was true and then asked me if I had seen her x-rays. He proceeded to say that he had never seen anything like it in all his life. He continued to say that my wife had so much cancer that he was flabbergasted that she was coherent and the fact that her blood work was normal was amazing. He ended by saying, "It's any day now." I told him that I didn't appreciate the way he spoke to my wife and that from now on if he had anything to say to my wife he would have to speak to me first. This doctor then told me that he did not subscribe to my theory and that people needed to know the truth. I answered back, "What do you know about truth to speak on the topic of death, you're not qualified to speak on this topic, next time you will speak with me only." I then walked away.

When I returned to the room I noticed a look of concern and worry on my wife's face, I could see that the words of the doctor had penetrated and were wearing heavily on her mind. My wife was having difficulty breathing and looked panicked and distressed. My wife choked out, "I can't breathe, I can't breathe, help me please." I tried to calm her by letting her know that everything was okay and to forget what the doctor had said. Her arms and legs began to flail uncontrollably; she looked like a drowning person gasping for air. I started to become very concerned as I was unable to calm her. I stepped outside the room and at the top of my lungs and in a panicked voice shouted, "We need help in here!" This immediately got the attention of staff and soon my wife was surrounded by paramedics and nurses.

As they entered the room they quickly realized the seriousness of the situation and pulled an oxygen mask from the wall and placed it directly on her face. This wasn't having any effect on my wife and as a result one of the nurses in charge called out, "Who has the power of attorney?" I responded that it was me and she quickly escorted me outside the room. She asked if I noticed the colour of my wife's lips and I told her that I had not. She then said that my wife's lips were blue which meant that she was not getting enough oxygen and considering her condition my wife may not pull through. The nurse then told me that this was going to be a very difficult night for me. I immediately reached for my cell phone and called my wife's brother to inform him that the situation was not good and that he needed to get to the hospital as soon as possible.

I returned to the room and could only watch as my wife was still in a complete panic state struggling to breathe. I knew from previous conversations with my wife that this was her worst fear of dying; suffocation and the inability to breathe. Nothing seemed to be helping at this point, and I'm not sure why, but I asked to take over from the nurse. Without hesitation the nurse allowed me to take hold of the oxygen mask and while holding it firmly against my wife's face I began to softly whisper in her ear the word love. In a gentle voice I continued to repeat the word love, love, love, love. Within minutes I could see that this was having a calming effect on her that I continued repeating the word love and then began adding the word god. I whispered; god's love god's love, god loves you, you are love, I love you, and love, love, love.

Her oxygen level slowly began rising and by the time her brother arrived at the hospital her oxygen level was remarkably back to normal. My wife had returned back to a calm state as I was beside myself questioning what had just unfolded before my eyes. I realized that I witnessed something remarkable and that I had just learned an important and valuable lesson about the power of words; words can have a positive or negative influence over things in life as was exemplified by the careless words of the doctor that almost ended a life while my words of love were able to restore and reverse its effect on that same life. I realized that the power of love cannot be overlooked or underestimated as a healing tool.

After this episode, my wife was admitted into the hospital and we again found ourselves back on the sixth floor. A lot of the nurses on the sixth floor remembered us and seemed surprised to see us back. My wife seemed somewhat different since her near death experience in the emergency ward. She seemed to be more appreciative of me and also somewhat subdued and humble. It was as if she had taken the first step toward surrendering to her circumstance.

Our new roommate arrived; she was in her early sixties and had lung cancer. To our dismay her oncologist was the same doctor that almost took my wife's life with his careless words. He was known as Dr. "D" in the hospital and "Dr. Death" to us. I know this may sound rather harsh, but consider what happened next to our new roommate when this same doctor came into contact with her.

We just finished celebrating this woman's birthday. She was in great spirits, she had a friend visiting and I overheard them talking about hope and taking things a day at a time, when all of a sudden Dr. D entered the room. He drew the curtain as if to have privacy to speak with her, yet, he spoke in a loud voice as he told her the results of her recent x-rays. This was what he said in a matter of fact way, "It's in god's hands now and I've been arguing with god all my life and I never win. All we can do is to try to keep you comfortable, okay." He then abruptly left the room. There was a few moments of silence after he left, then our roommate called out my name to see if I was still in the room. She asked me if I had heard what the doctor said and then asked me if I knew what he meant by his words. I saw that she was puzzled, but also shaken by his words. I tried to comfort her to no avail.

Later that evening, the roommate didn't seem herself. The expression on her face was unresponsive, devoid of any emotion, and zombie like; no longer did I see her bubbly personality. The next day her daughter arrived and was in shock at how different her mother was compared to the day before. She called the nurses, concerned for her mother. I let her know what took place when Dr. D paid her a visit. Sadly, they had to move her from our room because she wouldn't stop yelling throughout the night and she passed away two days later.

I recalled thinking to myself that the conduct of the doctor was so utterly disrespectful and irresponsible. Most anyone can learn the basic skills of medicine, but that doesn't make them a good doctor. I observed other instances where this same doctor released his "word bombs" and then left before witnessing the emotional carnage that he left behind. I brought this to the attention of other staff members at the hospital and they grinned. They told me that this was the doctor's style and that I needed to understand that he was from another generation. This was a poor excuse as far as I was concerned and I made it clear that he would no longer be welcome in our room. As a result of knowing truth beyond illusion, I offered hope to all those I met who were facing their worst fear, their mortality. Dr. D's words lacked any sense of compassion or understanding for what his patients were facing. His ignorance took away the only thing his patients had left to face their overwhelming circumstance. His parting gift was to substitute their self-worth, pride, dignity, hope, and courage with despair and hopelessness.

Living in a hospital setting day and night was an awakening experience for me. I witnessed a lot of suffering and not just from the patients but also from their families. I felt compelled to offer myself in any way I could to ease their pain. This was a side of me I had never known before. With my newly found spiritual approach I somehow instinctively knew who would be receptive and who would not be receptive to my words. I think that I was now being directed by my heart and not my mind and as a result I was experiencing the intelligence of my heart and trusting it power.

The more I witnessed death, the more comfortable I became with death. I knew that death was an illusion, similar to a magic trick. My main concern was how I could make people realize this without upsetting them. The answer to this question would come from a near death experience that my cousin went through over twenty years ago. When my cousin first told me about her near death experience, it went in one ear and out the other. I was young at the time and thought, "Cool, so what else is new with you?" It didn't faze me one bit. Twenty years later the experience of my cousin was profound and became a healing tool to ease the pain of those suffering.

The near death experience of my cousin Helena as expressed in her own unedited words:

It was New Year's Day 1984. After an evening of celebrating with family and friends, I was ready to have a much needed good night's rest. My son Ricky was fast asleep in his car seat but I managed to lay him in his crib without waking him. Finally I was out for the night. Around 2:30 am, I awoke with the strangest feeling in my throat and tongue. My arms were covered in hives; I leapt up to the bathroom mirror because my face began to throb. When I saw the reflection, I was horrified to see something from another planet looking back at me. My nose was flattened across my face and my lips were so swollen, they curled over my nostrils and chin. And my tongue throbbed so hard and had filled my mouth so that my upper and lower teeth couldn't touch. I could feel my throat closing up and my breath became more and more shallow. Because I lived alone with my son, the first person I thought of calling was my dad who lived a few blocks away. I screamed into the phone because I couldn't speak. After dropping the receiver, I stumbled to the side door to unlock it. My body fell hard to the floor as I took in my last wheezing breath.

Minutes seemed like hours but finally the door swung open and my parents had suddenly appeared in their pajamas. My mother holding her head and screaming at my dad to lift me off the floor and my dad yelling back at my mom to call 9-1-1, after the call, I remember her saying that she had urinated herself because of the nerves and panic she was feeling. My son at this point was crying hysterically in his crib and all I could concern myself with was to get my mom to go to his room and pick him up. My father tried repeatedly to lift my body off the floor but I was dead weight. I'm not sure how long it was before EMS showed up, but it seemed like hours.

Two people in uniform rushed in and immediately went to work. One took my pulse while the other turned me on my side and administered an injection into my thigh. Suddenly I found myself in the ambulance with an IV in my arm, an oxygen mask on my face and everyone yelling out orders. The siren was loud but the voices were piercing. I could feel my mind going into a peaceful state rather than the panic I was feeling earlier. The next thing I remember was waking up in the emergency room the next day. When my parents came to see me, my only concern was the wellbeing of my son. My mom couldn't believe that I was able to describe everything that had happened the night before like what my parents were wearing and what they were yelling at each other and also what the EMS men looked like and what they said and did. To my surprise, the two EMS attendants that, I'm guessing, saved my life, showed up to see how I was doing. Immediately I recognized and thanked them. They said it was impossible that I could know who they were because I was unconscious and so close to death. They told me I was very fortunate to recover so quickly. After going through all the events over and over again, I realized that there was no way that I could have known all the details. It suddenly occurred to me that I was watching everything unfold from above like looking out a second story window. I saw my body lying motionless while my parents ran around in a panic and my son standing up in his crib scared and crying to be picked up. The doctors assumed I had an allergic reaction to something I ate but to this day, I have no idea what it could have been. Years later, another similar incident happened to me during surgery. Apparently I'm allergic to penicillin. I found that out after an episode that I found myself watching my body jumping off the operating table with convulsions. Hearing "code blue" being yelled out in a room where it's you under the knife is a scary thought but for some reason I felt no panic this time, just peace. There is no doubt in my mind that there is life or something after death. If what you call my experiences an "out of body" thing or not, I know in my heart that I was at death's doorstep and for some reason I came back. Both times the doctors told me that I was very close to flat lining. I tell everyone that wants to know whether or not I believe in the afterlife....you bet I do!

We were approaching our sixth week in the hospital and once again there was a lot of pressure to move us out. Going home was out of the question and the only place left for us to go would be into a palliative unit. Knowing that this was the only alternative we had left, I had to find a way to convince my wife that going there had to do with hospital politics and not that she was expected to die soon.

When a person is sent to a palliative unit all treatment stops and it's about keeping a person comfortable until they pass. I insisted that the treatment continued in order to give my wife the impression that this was more about hospital politics. I had to convince my wife that this was the only place available for her to continue the long term treatment she required in a supportive environment. Going home was not an option for her and she did not want to go home, she felt safer in a hospital type setting.

Walking into a palliative unit for the first time felt surreal and eerie. As I passed the rooms I would look in with curiosity to see the faces of all the people waiting to die. It was a sad sight; many looked as if they were nervous frightened zombies. The rooms were bigger in the palliative unit than the ones at the hospital. There was a bed and a couple of chairs against the wall, a picture, and lots of empty space; this was a lifeless environment compared to that of the hospital we were in. I would best describe this as a kinder and quieter version of a solitary confinement in a prison.

Our room was located directly in front of the nursing station and our door was always wide open. This was an uncomfortable situation for us due to the constant loud laughter and joking that we were exposed to from some staff members as it freely entered and echoed through our room. I noticed that every time I looked out of our room there always seemed to be someone looking in with the same type of curiosity I had when we arrived.

By the third day I had enough and decided to be as impolite to them as I felt they were to us and closed the door. Given our situation, having people constantly peering in as they joked and laughed gave the impression that they were being inconsiderate. I don't believe that this was the case though, I felt there was more to this than met the eye. I believed this was their coping mechanism to remain indifferent and unaffected by their job. I guess if you don't know truth beyond the illusion of death, it must be very difficult to watch people die every day.

Doctor Berry was the Director of the palliative unit and he was as open minded as they come, without question he was the perfect fit for us. I remember the first time I met with him outside our room to discuss my wife's situation. He told me that he had reviewed her hospital medical records and that we were in the right place. He went on to say that according to her records he believed that she wouldn't be in the palliative unit for more than a week or two. I told him that I just finished paying for parking and I chose the monthly rate; he looked at me and said that he didn't think that was necessary. I then told him that we were going to be here a lot longer than that.

The will and determination of my wife to live was incredible. According to Dr. Berry, she had five times more cancer than anyone else and was taking five times less morphine than anyone else. My wife had maintained a daily record keeping system. She knew exactly what she ate, what pills she took, what time she took them, how many bowl movements she had, and even the type of movements she had. Dr. Berry told me that if there were ever a dispute over the medications between my wife and a nurse, he would side with my wife, because she was so meticulous and careful.

Living in a palliative unit was not easy. The only time I left the palliative unit was for my weekly sessions with Dr. Thornton. Dr.Thornton often encouraged me to write down my experiences and to use his Prayer Wheel Program. I had used his Prayer Wheel Program in the past and found it to be helpful, but I never wrote down my thoughts or answers to my questions. My circumstances were such now that I spent a lot of time in a room. I did have my long and exhausting days as well as days where my wife slept for long portions of the day. I decided that my time could have been better spent writing down my feelings and experiences into a note pad; I decided that I would give this a try.

It was a cloudy day and this seemed like the perfect day for me to try writing as my wife slept, so I took out my note book for the first time. I wanted to write my experiences down but didn't know where to start; I had never really written before. For some unexplained reason I used the Prayer Wheel Meditation technique to get started. Instead of just writing about my day I decided to write down whatever "popped" into my head and not question it. This is how the Prayer Wheel works and this is also how the "Assist Program" works. The Assist Program is another of Dr. Thornton's unconventional techniques used in his therapy.

This is what came to me at the time which turned out to be my first flow:

I am learning that during my difficult and challenging times, it is your inner voice, your higher self, and your heart where guidance lies. This gives balance during difficult times. Understanding your situation from a spiritual perspective gives you balance by knowing truth. Truth brings calm to a situation. Without truth, fear and confusion set in. Truth and knowledge bring understanding and calms the situation. Fear will drain your energy and doesn't help those that need your help. People who are suffering need care and compassion. Fear will only put distance between you and the one that is suffering. Balance doesn't mean that you won't feel pain in the midst of turmoil. Balance allows you to understand what's really going on, enabling you to flow through the experience with a degree of calm, interjecting light into the situation and dissolving the darkness. Your inner voice message is your personal guidance. Don't fear your inner voice. Have no fear, step outside the box of your mind's eye. If you become caught up in the negative aspects of what is happening, not being able to see beyond the pain and suffering at hand, then you'll become bound by them. This is your opportunity to connect to the mission of your soul to overcome past mistakes, to free yourself from your past and awaken to the truth. Have no fear and connect to your heart and allow the light of truth to serve you and to free you. Do not fear your heart, trust your heart, and trust your journey.

During my next session with Dr. Thornton, I brought my note book and read what had come to me. I wondered if he would think perhaps that it was juvenile and poorly written. To my surprise, Dr. Thornton thought it was well written. I asked him if he really thought this was good and if it made sense to him. Dr. Thornton responded by telling me that it absolutely made sense. I told him that I didn't know why it came out this way but that probably it was because I chose to use the Prayer Wheel technique. Dr. Thornton encouraged me to continue writing.

It was a Saturday evening and the night nurse entered the room doing her usual rounds. As she was leaving the room she unexpectedly stopped, turned and asked me if I would have some free time the following day to speak with her. Without hesitation, I told her that I would and as she turned to leave I called out her name and asked her what she wanted to discuss with me. She replied with one word, "forgiveness" and then left the room. My wife, with a puzzled look on her face questioned, "What do you know about forgiveness?" I responded with telling her that the nurse seemed to think I knew something about it. I then turned to my wife and told her that in fact I would try and write a flow on forgiveness using the Prayer Wheel techniques; I would just write down whatever came to me. My wife responded with concern by telling me not to make a fool of myself.

On the following Sunday morning as my wife was still asleep I pulled out my notebook and began writing by using the Prayer Wheel technique. An hour or so later I had my forgiveness flow completed. When my wife awoke, I asked her if she'd like me to read my forgiveness flow to her but she was too tired. Later that day the nurse entered the room and after attending to my wife asked me if we could go to the rest area to talk. We had a seat and I told her that I didn't know what it was that she wanted to talk to me about, but I asked her to allow me to first read something that I wrote on forgiveness. She agreed to this and I read the following flow to her:

What is the meaning of forgiveness? Do we understand the power of forgiveness? Do you consider forgiveness to be a sign of weakness or a sign of strength? Who benefits from forgiveness? True forgiveness comes from the heart. That's where we find unconditional forgiveness. To forgive and not forget is not from the heart; this is not unconditional forgiveness. This kind of forgiveness is of the mind. This is ego holding on to the past. True forgiveness releases you from the past, removing the dark matter of hurt from your soul. Unconditional forgiveness will remove the stress from your body, allowing your cells to vibrate in balance. Unconditional forgiveness is necessary to bring closure to a karmic lesson manifested from a previous life experience. Unconditional forgiveness removes the sting in your heart and brings warmth to your heart in the present moment. Every day, take a minute to send forgiveness to all those who have hurt you or taken advantage of you by calling on their soul. Say, dear soul of (person's name), I love you, I forgive you unconditionally. Thank you for your service to me and for allowing me the opportunity to practice forgiveness. Then chant, Gods Love, Gods Love, Gods Love. While chanting, visualize a white light surrounding that person or persons with peace, love, and unconditional forgiveness. Follow your heart and listen to your heart for it knows truth. Have no fear; forgiveness is love. Forgiveness starts with self; love thyself for you are perfect. Forgive thy mistakes, for they are blessings that serve to teach us about love. Your ego wants you to fear forgiveness, to see it as a sign of weakness, giving in, and accepting defeat. Listen to your heart; trust your heart for it knows truth. God forgives; do you consider God to be weak? Awaken to the truth that is within you. Be strong, be love, be your true-self your god-self: forgive, forgive, forgive, and heal, heal, heal.

I finished reading my flow to the nurse and noticed tears in her eyes. She then began to open up to me about her situation and then suddenly ended the conversation by saying, "Yep, okay, got it, I know what to do now, thank you." She then got up from the couch and started to leave the area. I rose from my chair and positioned myself in front of her to prevent her from leaving. I asked her if she was okay and she gave me a hug and said that she was fine.

The next day, while the nurse was doing her rounds, she entered our room as usual with no mention of our conversation the day before. She quietly did her usual work routine and as she was leaving the room, she stopped, turned around, and burst into tears while saying, "My heart thanks you." I was completely caught off guard by her comment and it penetrated deeply into my heart which caused my eyes to well with tears. This was the first sign and validation to me that my flows had meaning. After she left the room, I turned to my wife and said, "Looks like I didn't make a fool of myself after all."

The rooms around us kept emptying; every day I made a point to look at the wall board in the hallway to see the names of the patients. The names changed almost daily. One minute you're talking to a patient and then the next minute they collapse on the floor and are pronounced dead. It is the oddest thing to see someone walking perfectly fine and the next minute falling face down.

I recall hearing a man talking and laughing with the nurses in front of the nurse's station; he seemed to be in good spirits, clearly doing far better than my wife who was confined to a bed. As he made his way back to his room there was a loud thump sound and I knew he had passed without warning.

Eight weeks had passed and the staff couldn't believe that my wife was still alive. All the rooms around us had already emptied at least twice. The Director of the palliative unit called me aside to discuss my wife's situation. He asked if we would consider going home as he felt that my wife seemed to be strong and stable enough to go home and commented that she was a fighter. He also said that he'd never seen anything like this before having had thousands of patients. He then remarked that if someone were to see her x-rays they would agree that she shouldn't be alive. After listening to what the director had to say, I told him that I disagreed with his assertion that she was stable enough to go home. I asked that my wife not be moved from the palliative unit. I went on to say that change would be very difficult for her to handle at this point. I was grateful that the director demonstrated having compassion in my circumstance as he willingly agreed to fight for my wife, if need be, to allow her to stay as long as required.

Sixteen weeks had now passed and the flowers were now in bloom. It was the last week in May and oh how I longed to be outside. I was looking out of the window; there wasn't a cloud in the sky as far as the eye could see. For some unexplained reason, I looked straight up; this was something that I would not normally do. I got a glimpse of something white in the sky and I leaned and pressed up against the window to get a better look. Straight up above, I noticed a small cloud, the only cloud in the sky. I realized that the odds of my seeing this cloud were next to impossible if I had not looked straight up, and I do mean straight up.

It was rather strange to be so captivated by a small white cloud, and an unusual thought entered my mind at that time telling me not to look away and to keep my eyes focused on the cloud because there was a message for me. Crazy as this may appear; I had an unexplained knowing within me to follow and trust this guidance. As I focused my complete attention on the cloud I noticed that it did not move and remained in the same spot while constantly changing its shape until it slowly dissipated to nothing. The next thought I had was to write down whatever came to me without question or fear.

The following is the ensuing flow that came to me on May 28, 2008:

Prayer Wheel Flow
On
Lessons from a Little White Cloud

Here I am, sitting in a palliative care unit staring out of my window into a clear blue sky. A beautiful little white cloud appeared before my eyes. The cloud began to slowly dissipate. The cloud eventually vanished before my eyes, and a thought entered my mind "Was this the death of a cloud, for I have an empty feeling inside now that it's gone?" The cloud was in constant motion, constantly changing its shape, slowly transforming from a physical state of matter to an invisible state of energy. I slowly began to realize that this was not the death of a cloud, but the rebirth of a cloud into another dimension. A rebirth into another realm, and that life is about constant change, and that I, also being life, am about constant change; nothing ever remains the same. Death is rebirth and rebirth is change. Death must not be seen as an end, but as a new beginning. This tiny cloud served me well today, for it showed me that life does not die, life constantly changes and we must learn to let go of the empty feeling that follows change; the empty feeling which follows a loved one's transition, and a loved one's rebirth into another realm. For the separation we feel is only a physical illusion, and in reality, separation has not taken place; the love always stays with us. Love and life are one and the same, love and life are eternal, and love and life link all souls, all spirits together and forever to the greater spirit of god. I will always remember this beautiful little white cloud. Thank you for showing me that life does not know death and that life is about new beginnings and never ending changes.

I continued to write my flows as I found this to be therapeutic and it helped pass the time. As my wife now slept most of the days away, I couldn't help but wonder what was going on when I looked around the room. She refused to pass on and in a sense seemed to be watching over me as she slept; kind of like overseeing me as I spent my days writing in the midst of her suffering. It was as if this palliative room was my spiritual classroom of knowledge, wisdom, and truth and she was my spiritual teacher. This brought me to the realization that speaking words aloud are not needed in order to teach on a spiritual level, and that an experience speaks louder and deeper than any word can.

I also realized that I had a choice to accept or to deny this experience, this, as a thought entered my mind and told me not to go into fear; to face fear and to be still to allow the fear to move through me and discover a higher truth. I embraced this wisdom and exposed fear to be nothing more than a bully while the only power fear truly has is the power we give it, and when we stand up to fear it will disappear into the night.

My wife was no longer able to face her situation; she preferred to take a pill and sleep her days away. She had become more submissive and quiet, and I suspected that she had become tired of fighting. My wife was quietly letting go and accepting her reality; she requested that I hold her hand every night until she fell asleep.

My wife had bone fractures in her neck, arms, and in her legs. Her stomach was distended, her lungs were full of fluid, and you could hear gurgitation as she breathed. She had cancer protruding through certain areas of her skin and her spinal column had collapsed. My wife had bone pain throughout her entire body and I could understand how she would rather sleep than face this pain minute by minute. Dr. Berry could not believe her determination. He told me that he had thousands of patients that came through his unit and he had never seen anything like this.

We were nearing the end of July, 2008 and my wife felt a sharp pain in her head. Soon after, I noticed that she was not making sense when she spoke. My wife asked me for her lip balm and instead of applying it to her lips she applied the balm to her tongue. I intervened and like a child who wanted to keep her toy, she held the balm firmly in her grasp and refused to let it go. I found myself having to negotiate and I offered her a drink on the condition that she let go of the balm in her hand. She agreed and opened up her hand allowing me to take it.

Oddly enough, I was relieved that the cancer had gone to her brain. My wife no longer understood her situation, and therefore, her suffering had ended. She was now like a four year old child. When the nurses entered the room since this change in my wife's condition, they were deeply saddened. Even though they were saddened and I saw the tears in their eyes, they couldn't help but laugh at all the cute and funny things that would come out of her mouth, like the expression, "Out of the mouths of Babes."

In a very short period of time my wife lost her ability to speak, she just mumbled to herself all day long. She also needed to have something in her hand to fidget with, usually a piece of tissue, and she would fidget with this all day long. My wife was in her own little world now. This was sad to witness and yet I was relieved and comforted by the knowledge that she was no longer suffering. For years I was under a constant daily pressure to keep her calm, hopeful, and at peace. It was a challenge to keep her positive and living in the moment, and now it was over. The end of her physical life was nearing and I could sense it.

Remarkably, I noticed another interesting and unexplained shift in my wife's abilities. My wife was now able to put together sentences and phrases that demonstrated a level of comprehension once again. I noticed this when my wife told me that she was seeing spirits in the room. One day, as I was about to seat myself, she told me not to sit in that particular chair as the seat was saved for "them." I quietly asked my wife, "Who is 'them'?" My wife replied with, "the angels."

On another occasion, my wife was trying to get my attention as I sat by the window. I couldn't hear her, but I could tell that she was whispering and motioning me to come to her side. I then went to her side and quietly asked her what she wanted. She said that there were two men in the room and I asked her where these men were. She told me that they were over there and she pointed. Something told me to open up and accept this possibility as her sudden coherency from a childlike state, where she made no sense at all was unexplainable. This coherency was however sporadic, limited, and appeared to be on her terms only. This coherency was limited to these spiritual experiences only and was initiated by her. I asked my wife if she knew who these men were. Quietly, she whispered to me and said yes while raising her hand and giving them a childlike wave. My wife had a peaceful smile upon her face and it was as if she were in another world. I asked my wife if the men were good men or bad men; she told me that they were good men. I asked her what these men wanted, and she told me that they wanted to take her to the "miracle station" when she was ready. My wife further told me that they wanted her to leave in the evening. These conversations between my wife and the angels continued for a few days.

One of the last visions my wife had as I sat by the window was a sudden burst of excitement, she exclaimed, "Look, look by the window!" I looked at the window, but didn't see anything. I asked her what she was seeing and she burst out again "Look, look, by the window…wow!" I walked over to her bed and again asked what she was seeing. She told me that there were flower birds, birds of flower by the window, and that they were so beautiful. I repeated what she had said to me, "flower birds, but I can't see them." My wife then told me to put my glasses on and went on to say that there were golden and silver birds, and that her favourite ones were the golden birds of flower.

A few more days had passed and my wife's eyes were now completely closed and she was no longer able to respond or communicate. She was in an unconscious state. As a result, the doctors were unable to gauge her pain level and decided to just maintain her current pain dosage. I attempted to feed her water through a straw. It was quite amazing how she was unable to open her eyes or communicate, and yet, when she sensed the straw touch her lips, she would instinctively suck on the straw.

It was around 4:00 am and I couldn't sleep, so, I got up and went to sit by the window. At one point, I decided to give my wife a drink and what happened next was unbelievable. My wife, with her eyes closed, gently whispered my name and gave me what I knew to be a spiritual message. I got goose bumps as she spoke; I instantly knew that this message was not coming from her, the person, but rather the soul. My wife was not one to ever speak in this manner. This is what she said, "Tony, you are coming back four more times, I don't know what part of the world, because it will depend on…." (She mumbled the last word). I immediately responded by asking her, "Depends on what, depends on what?" There was no response. I decided to write down this message in order not to forget it.

Thirty minutes or so had passed and I went over to give my wife another drink, all of a sudden she whispered my name and repeated what she had said before word-perfect; it felt as if I was listening to a recording. She used the same pitch, the same wording, the same inflection, and again I got goose bumps.

I received more spiritual messages over the next couple of days. One of the more profound messages I received was the reason as to why my wife was in my life and enduring suffering against all odds. Again, my wife's message was delivered in the exact same manner as all the rest; in a whispered voice with her eyes closed. Her voice was as though she was disclosing a secret. It was a soft, peaceful, maternal whisper, unlike any I'd ever heard before. This is what she said, "Tony, I want to lift your service." When I heard this, I intuitively knew that this was connected to the previous message when she mumbled the last word. The last part of that message would have ended this way: it will depend on….. "Service."

One of the last messages I received from my wife was this: "Tony, don't be irritated by people." She then said, “Tony, write a book.” When I heard this, I repeatedly responded by asking her what I should write about; there was no response. Then approximately twenty minutes later, I heard my wife speak again in a whispered voice; with her eyes closed she said one word, “ME.” In my attempt to understand what she meant by this, I asked her what I would write about regarding her; there was no response.

It was now August 10, 2008, and I was awakened at 3:00 am by a loud noise. There was a very loud groan, grunt type sound coming from my wife every time she exhaled. Her eyes were closed, her teeth were clenched tight, and her heart was beating unbelievably fast. I knew this because I pressed my ear to her chest and I felt what I could only describe as a heartbeat that was not humanly possible. The closest analogy, although not exact, would be to describe it as a piston of a car engine revving. There was no interrupting this relentless, robotic grunt. It was so loud that I had to cover my ears with my hands every now and then. No one seemed to know what was causing this. The grunts were relentless and physically and humanly impossible for anyone to sustain; anyone else would have tired after about 10-20 minutes. By the time her parents called to see how things were it was 11:00 am, and I was at my wits end. Eight hours had passed and my wife was still grunting strong with every exhale and there was no end in sight.

I warned my wife's parents of what to expect when they arrived. At approximately 1:00 pm her parents arrived to witness for themselves what I had been enduring now for the past ten hours. Her mother covered her ears and was visibly shaken by this new turn of events. After about three hours or so, this situation became too difficult and unbearable for her parents. I told them both to go home and eat something; I was hoping that by the time they returned, things would have settled down.

After my wife's parents left, the Director of the palliative unit, Dr. Berry came to see me as I had requested his presence. He stood by the bedside of my wife with a perplexed look on his face. Dr. Berry told me that in all of his years working in a palliative environment, he had never witnessed such a thing. Dr. Berry was somewhat awestruck by what he was witnessing. He commented to me that this was both amazing and unbelievable. He could not offer any explanation and he thanked me for bringing this to his attention before leaving the room.

I was left alone in the room and one of the nurses entered to speak with me, the nurse wanted to ask my permission to have a priest give my wife some sort of blessing. The nurse told me that she considered my wife to be a friend, and as a friend, she wanted to have a priest come to bless my wife. She then told me that she was Catholic, and she asked me what my denomination was. I explained to her, that although I was raised as Catholic, I was not a practicing Catholic. I told the nurse that I was okay with her having a priest come to give the blessing, but added that I didn't really think this would do anything. Since, it was a gesture of compassion and kindness, I told the nurse she should go ahead and do this. The nurse thanked me and left the room to call the Chaplain.

There was a knock at the door and a man peered into the room and asked if it was okay to come in. I invited him in and he introduced himself. He let me know that he was the hospital Chaplain and that one of the nurses had asked him to give a blessing to my wife. He had a look of trepidation and seemed rather nervous. My guess was that he was briefed by the nurse and she must have told him that I was not religious. As well, it was possibly the loud grunting coming from my wife. I'm sure that this was not something he had ever witnessed either.

After the blessing was performed, I thanked the Chaplain and he turned to me and said, "I heard that you have been here alone in this room for quite some time, it must be very difficult not to have someone to talk with." I told him that it wasn't that difficult because I had occupied my time with writing. The Chaplain then asked me what I had been writing about, and I told him that I was writing about life and the spiritual messages that my wife had given me.

The Chaplain was curious and wanted to know more, the next thing I knew, I had been rambling on for over half an hour.

Having realized this, I abruptly stopped myself mid-sentence. The Chaplain asked me why I stopped with a puzzled expression on his face. I told him that I just realized that I had been talking at him and not with him for over half an hour. The Chaplain told me that there was no need to stop, and that he had been enjoying listening and had heard every word that I said. I couldn't help but think to myself that I was speaking to a Chaplain in such a way that contradicts some of the teachings of Catholicism. The Chaplain, to my surprise appeared captivated and not at all offended. He wanted to hear more, so I read him one of my recent flows. After I finished reading the flow, the Chaplain responded with a sense of wonderment, he told me that the flow was powerful. The following is the flow I read to him that day:

Prayer Wheel Flow
On
Freewill

Freewill is not perfect and is not imperfect; Freewill is perfect imperfection. Freewill is an ideal flaw, and freewill is a timeless, eternal opportunity to continually increase, develop, and express our true spiritual qualities. Unlimited Freewill does not exist in the physical world of matter, and does not exist in the spiritual world of thought. For all is governed by spiritual natural law, and laws within laws. The planets and all of nature are governed by natural law, and man is no exception. Man, having a soul, mind, and body, is governed by spiritual and physical natural law. Natural law influences and limits the Freewill of man. If natural law did not exist, the entire universe, including man, would live in total chaos. For you are an evolving developing soul having had repeated physical life experiences. These experiences define your present character, your mental development, and present spiritual development. For all are free to steal, cheat, and to kill; yet many do not. Their previous life experiences have raised their soul consciousness and their inner sense of right and wrong to a level which prevents them from stealing, cheating, and from killing. The soul is in charge and the physical life purpose is decided before incarnation. Therefore, Freewill is limited to one's physical life purpose. Freewill is your eternal everlasting gift which allows you to find closure to past life mistakes and create anew. Freewill is an opportunity to discover the qualities of the greater spirit within. Life, through Freewill, allows the opportunity to uplift or lessen the evolution of your soul. Freewill is a key to unlock the imprisoned soul to ascend beyond the physical world of matter to experience the magical world of infinite thought.

T.S. August 8, 2008

It was now 7:30 pm and the dark of night was fast approaching. My wife's situation had not changed all day. She continued to grunt with every exhale. It was surreal; there were no words to describe what this experience felt like. For me, sitting alone in that room, exposed to the relentless, loud, grunting for that length of time was nothing short of torturous. I thought to myself, how was this possible; my wife had been grunting robotically, uninterrupted for seventeen hours with her eyes closed, her teeth clenched, and her heart still beating as fast as it had been before. This was beyond comprehension and humanly impossible. Clearly, my wife was not in a lucid, coherent state by any means; yet, she very clearly articulated the word "sorry" twice within two of the exhaling grunts, and resumed her uninterrupted robotic grunting. This suggested to me that there was a level of consciousness within the incomprehensive state she was in. My thoughts then turned to why this happened now; I wondered why my wife uttered the word "sorry" at this time. A half hour had passed since this incident, I finally couldn't take it anymore; I had reached my breaking point. I raised both my arms up toward the ceiling and while looking up said, "Please, enough....she has suffered enough." I then looked at my wife and whispered to her, "it's okay, you can leave now, I will be alright." Then, like magic, within seconds the robotic grunting stopped. The room fell silent for the first time in seventeen hours. I couldn't believe it and I looked up toward the ceiling and said, "Thank you god."

A minute or so passed since my wife stopped grunting, and I could see that she was still breathing. Then all of a sudden I heard a gurgle type sound. I rushed over to her side; it looked as if she had stopped breathing. I leaned in to listen and simultaneously placed my hand upon her chest. She didn’t appear to be breathing and there was no sign of a heartbeat. All of a sudden there was a powerful gasp and an explosive expansion of her chest, so powerful that my hand flew off her chest. This was immediately followed by a calm still which was surreal. I wondered if that was her final breath and if she had passed away.

I quickly made my way to the nurse’s station and explained what had happened and the nurse rushed to the room. The nurse took one look at my wife and fell apart; she began to cry and said, “I didn’t want this to happen on my shift, not my shift!” The word spread quickly to the other nurses.

Soon after my wife passed away, her parents arrived and upon entering the room, her mother fell to her knees. She was immediately surrounded by nurses; they were all hugging and crying as one; if a stranger were to enter the room they would not know who the grieving mother was. Being mothers themselves, the nurses felt the pain of my mother in law.

One of the first calls I made after my wife passed away was to Dr. Thornton. He asked me how I was doing and I told him that I had a feeling of satisfaction as well as relief. I told him that I felt a sense of satisfaction because I knew I did the right thing by seeing this through to the end, and that I also felt a sense of relief because I knew that my wife's suffering had ended.

I spent that entire night and the following day mostly alone with my wife. The hours were spent analyzing and questioning what had happened. I walked over to my wife's body to touch her many times; I wanted to see how her body felt now compared to when there was life in it. Each time I could feel the emptiness, I knew without a doubt that her body was merely a vehicle and not the “real” person.

Standing next to a lifeless body felt like standing next to a piece of furniture. I was at peace now, knowing the truth that life does not end.

As I continued to move forward on this journey, people questioned my calm state, especially at the funeral. I would let those individuals know that the reason for my calm state was because I knew truth and truth sets you free. Death seems real, but is it? I learned that what is real never dies, and the coming months would only solidify and confirm my new found wisdom.

When someone passes away, the family longs for a sign to know that their loved one is okay. The types of thoughts that run through their minds are: Where are you, and are you at peace? Can you see me and can you hear me? Please give me a sign so I will know. I was no different; I had asked those same questions. I wondered if I would receive a sign that my wife was okay and I did in fact receive a sign. I didn't receive an ambiguous sign of which I had to convince myself; I in fact received two signs consistently over a long period of time with physical evidence.

These signs started approximately one month after the passing of my wife. I've always liked music throughout my life, but this time music took on a whole new meaning for me. I found that music had a spiritual relevance and substance; music had more meaning to me now. This was something that I never experienced before. When I listen to music now, regardless of the genre, I feel a sense of peace and contentment. I like listening to jazz, soft rock, heavy metal, classical rock, some pop, and seventies music.

I came across an internet radio website called theradio.com. There are lots of stations to choose from and my station of choice was Crush Radio which played alternative rock with some classic rock. I would listen to this station regularly while surfing the net. One day, a song came on that didn't fit the Crush Radio genre. It was a Whitney Houston song called, I will always love you. I was about to click the forward icon to skip this song, when all of a sudden something occurred to me. I realized that this wasn't just any song; it was a special song that my wife left me.

A few years before my wife passed away, we were driving in the car and a Whitney Houston song came on the radio. My wife turned to me and said, “You know, when I hear this song it makes me think about us and all the things that are going on in our lives. If I were to leave you, this would be the song I would leave you with." I thought it was on odd thing for her to say at the time and feeling uncomfortable, I decided to ignore this. We did not discuss this song again and the topic did not come up again.

As I listened to this song now playing on the internet, I paid attention to the words for the first time and the words brought tears to my eyes. I couldn’t believe that this was happening to me and I thought that this was a coincidence. I heard this song again the following day and eventually I began to hear this song multiple times per day on a regular basis. This went on for a few months and was not limited to theradio.com. I would hear it in shopping centres, the car radio, on TV and I rarely watched TV. I knew this was odd, but I was so used to it that I didn’t think much of it until an unbelievable and unforeseen turn of events.

I was visiting with my sister and it was getting late. My sister went to bed and I stayed up to surf the net and to check my e-mails. I was listening to theradio.com and I heard the Whitney Houston song again. I smiled and I thought to myself, there’s that song again. When I finished checking my e-mails, I logged out and closed the window. The theradio.com was now the only window open and I noticed that the screen looked different. There appeared to be no problems with the website except that the page looked different. There was a white image frozen on the screen with some writing. I thought of logging off and then getting back on to see if this would correct the problem, when I noticed what was repeatedly written within the white image on the screen. This is what I saw: Whitney Houston “I will always love you” Whitney Houston “I will always love you. Whitney Houston “I will always love you." I was amazed and at the same time, considering everything that had happened to me, on some level I was not surprised.

I immediately rushed upstairs and startled my sister who was sleeping. I told her to hurry and come downstairs to see something. My sister sat up immediately and said, "What is it, what happened?"

I told her to come quickly because what I wanted to show her may be gone. We quickly rushed down the stairs and when we got to the computer, I was relieved and surprised to see that the image was still there. I told my sister to look at the computer as I pointed to the image on the screen. My sister asked me what she was looking for and I told her to look at the screen closely. She looked at the screen more closely and told me that the screen appeared to be frozen or something. I told her to read what was written and she repeated the words on the screen back to me, "Whitney Houston, I will always love you. Whitney Houston, I will always love you." My sister then said, "Yeah, so what?" I responded by telling her how this song came into my life and that years ago my wife told me that if she were to leave me this would be the song she would leave me with. I told her that since my wife passed away, I was hearing this very song many times per day. After explaining this to my sister, she became excited and told me to get a picture of the screen because no one would believe this. My sister went back upstairs to wake her husband. My bother-in-law came downstairs with somewhat of a skeptical look on his face. I'm sure he thought this was weird, but he didn't say a word about it. He took a couple of pictures with his camera and went back to bed.

I noticed something quite incredible the following day when I was looking at the pictures. Remember, how I mentioned that my wife told me that if she were to leave me, this would be the song that she would leave me with. Well, incredibly at the same time that my brother-in-law took the picture, there was a song playing and the name of the song playing at the time was, "Babe, I'm gonna leave You" by Led Zeppelin. If you look closely at the picture of theradio.com screen on the next page you will notice that a part of this title was captured as it was scrolling in the area of the window that names the song. That part of the title in the window shows as: Gonna Leave You;" Led Zeppelin. My rational mind wanted me to believe that this was a coincidence, but deep down I knew it was wasn't; this was a message from my wife. I owe a big thanks to my sister as I probably would not have taken these pictures.

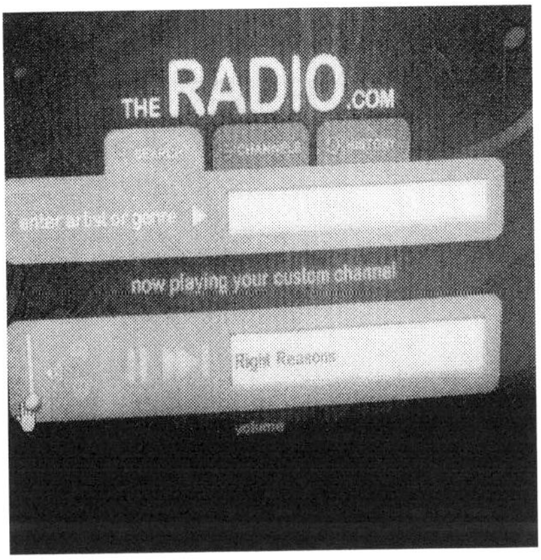

The RADIO.com "normal" computer screen photo

The RADIO.com "paranormal" computer screen photo

It was now June 19, 2009 and this was our wedding anniversary, the first anniversary since my wife's passing. I was wondering when I'd get another message from my wife. I had the distinct feeling that this would happen, due to all that had transpired and how important "dates" were to my wife. My instincts were right; my wife did send me a message, only I didn't know it at the time. This message I received took place when I was in Niagara Falls with my family to celebrate Father's Day.

My family and I decided to separate and do our own thing; we had set up a time to meet later that evening. It was getting late and I didn't hear from them, so I decided to give them a call. I reached for my cell phone and noticed I had received a text message with a blank subject line. I thought this was rather odd, so I opened it and there was a message. The text message read: "12:00 am 31 Dec 10." I realized that this was an interesting way of saying the year 2011. This definitely got my attention and I got goose bumps, I believed that this was in fact a message from my wife.

I knew my cell phone plan automatically deleted all voice messages and all text messages within five days, so I was interested to see what, if anything would happen to this anonymous text message. Five days had passed and as expected, all my text messages deleted automatically, except for this anonymous text message that was received on our wedding anniversary. I couldn't help but wonder what this message could possibly mean. I wondered if she was trying to warn me that something bad was going to happen to me or perhaps something bad was going to take place somewhere in the world. If this was in fact a message from my wife, I wondered why she didn't just say I'm okay, instead of giving an ambiguous date. I believed that in time I would receive the answer.

One week passed and the message was still there on my cell phone. Now one month had passed and the message was still there on my phone. As the months now turned to a year the message was still there on my phone. It was, in fact, the only text message that had not been automatically deleted after five days. I knew that I needed to get a picture of this. I had a friend who is a photographer; he has a spiritual nature and is open minded to things like this. I asked him if he would mind taking a picture of my cell phone which he agreed to.

My cell phone was old and out-dated; I was in desperate need of a new phone, but felt the need to wait until the message date had passed. I wanted to see what would happen with my phone, if anything. I thought perhaps I would get a follow up message that would explain this ambiguous text message further.

There was another reason that this text message got my attention. All my life, I have been surrounded by the number 11, or 1:11 or 11:11. I first noticed this number when I was a child, and this would usually happen when I was in bed. If I was having difficulty sleeping and I'd look at the clock it would, more often than not, read 11:11 or 1:11. This happened so often that it became somewhat of a game to me; I'd wake up suddenly tossing and turning and I'd look to see what time it was. Now knowing the odds of seeing this number eleven, I would slowly open one eye, only to take a peek, while saying to myself; "I bet it will be 11:11" and nine times out of ten it was 11:11.

Having seen this number or combination of this number so often as a child it suddenly and without notice stopped. Going into adulthood, I had forgotten about this number; it no longer had relevance to me. Now, twenty years later as I was driving in my car, I noticed the time showing on the clock was 1:11 and this number began to appear repeatedly. So much so, that it got my attention again and I started getting flashbacks to when I was a child, and I decided to share this silly childhood story with my wife. My wife surmised that I was probably seeing this number repeatedly because I was looking for it or thinking about it. The truth is, I don't wake up thinking about this number and I don't walk around thinking about it, this number just seems to surround me. Within a very short period of time my wife also started seeing this number on a regular basis. When I sarcastically told her that this was because she was probably looking for it or thinking about it, she told me that she wasn't and that it was starting to freak her out!

One day, as I was driving to my warehouse, my wife and I noticed that the time in the car was showing as 1:11 pm. Pointing to the clock, I showed my wife that number again. We arrived at our warehouse and got out of the car, and we walked up to the door when I noticed a bunch of pennies on the ground. I turned to my wife and said, "Who would drop a bunch of pennies by the door and just leave them there?" I picked them up before entering the warehouse and threw the pennies into the cash register.

About six months later, the exact same thing happened. As I was approaching the front door of my warehouse, I saw a bunch of pennies on the ground. I was thinking that this was very odd, especially since this happened before. I scooped up the pennies and just before I was about to throw them into the cash register, I stopped and said to my wife, "What do you think the odds are that I'm holding eleven pennies in my hand?" I proceeded to count the pennies one by one and sure enough there was eleven pennies!

We both saw that number daily and it wasn't just on a clock. We saw it on license plates, addresses, documents, and room numbers assigned to us in thc hospital. We were surrounded by this number, so much so, that my wife began to feel it was an omen, a sign of sorts and made me cover any and all digital clocks.

Since this number eleven played a significant role in my wife's life, I wondered if it was also hidden within the cryptic text message on my cell phone. I came to the realization that if you added up the text message numbers, the total would equal eleven. To illustrate this, you would have to take the text message and convert the abbreviation Dec. to its number value of 12. The text message (12 am 31 Dec 10) converted would look like this (12:00 31 12 10) and when added together would read as: 1+2+0+0+3+1+1+2+1+0=11. This cryptic text message was an interesting way of indicating the year 2011. I knew deep within me that this could only have come from my late wife and from no other source.

A year and a half had now passed since I received this phone text. The message was still there in spite of the fact that all other subsequent text messages had automatically deleted within five days. It was New Year's Eve, 2010 and this was the moment that I had been waiting for. I wondered what was going to happen if anything and I wondered if there would be another text message. When the clock struck 12:00 am I looked at my phone and nothing had changed.

Later that morning, I turned on the television to see if anything significant had taken place in the world but nothing unusual had occurred. The next morning I checked my phone and the original message was still there. Later that evening, I checked my phone again and to my surprise the message had suddenly disappeared. I couldn't believe the text message simply vanished from my phone a year and a half later; one day into the year of 2011. As it would turn out, 2011 did mark the beginning of what was to be a significant change in my life circumstance which involved the lifting of service to others. My ability to discern truth became heightened to a level which superseded my experience in life. This "lifting of service" was one of the messages given to me by my wife when she was in a coma state before she passed. The spiritual message bestowed on me was, "I want to lift your service."

The next week, I spoke with Dr. Thornton and explained what had happened and he told me that I should do a flow. The following are the pictures of my cell phone that depict the anonymous text message and a flow on the significance of this follows on the next page. I have also written a flow on the significance of the number eleven eleven on page 77.

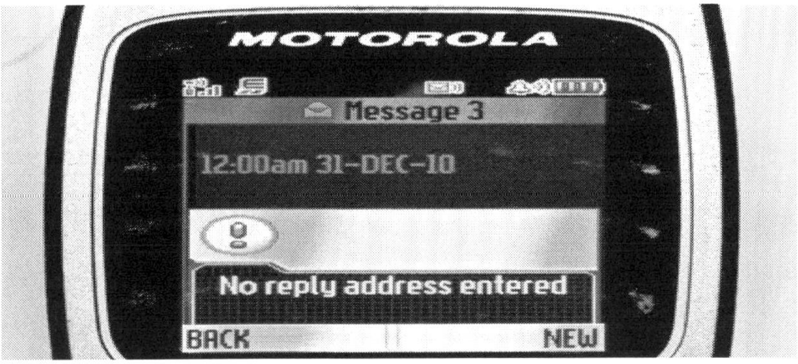

Text message received. Photo by Greg Dru from Druworx Photography

#3 Inbox Message is a blank space. Photo by Greg Dru from Druworx

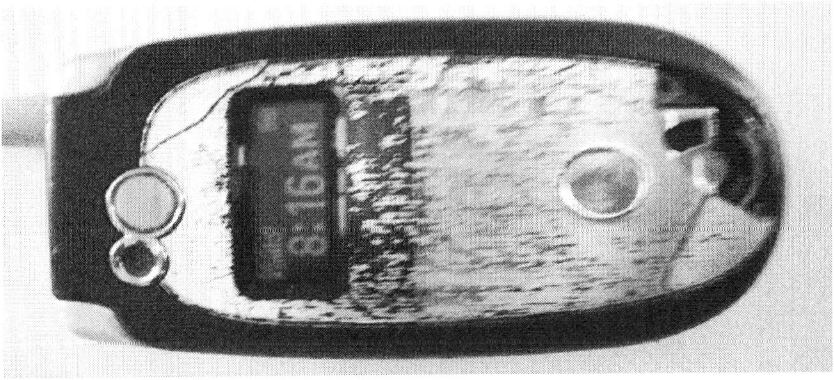

Phone condition a year and a half later

Prayer Wheel Flow
Universal Love

Outside of physical love and beyond romantic love exists universal love. For this is a selfless love which serves unconditionally, for this is a humble love which serves respectfully, and this is an intelligent love which is knowledgeable and experienced. The unconditional purpose behind universal love is to stimulate, awaken, and lift the service of others in order to realize their true self. Universal love can only be obtained through service to others. Universal love is inseparable and attainable as a collective love; for it cannot be achieved by oneself alone. The steps that make up the ladder toward universal love are the rungs of service taken from each lifetime. In order to lift oneself up to the next level, one must at the same time reach down and lift up those from the rungs below. Service to others is how one acquires the knowledge and experience necessary to progress. Each rung on the ladder represents a completion of service. With each rung of service completed, there is a further awakening to one's true self and there is a further awakening to unconditional service. Unconditional service is the higher ascension toward unconditional love, for it is the higher ascension toward ones earthly graduation. Unconditional service does not end with one's final transition; there is no separation between the physical and the spiritual. The higher ascensions of one ladder are the lower ascensions of another.

On November 10, 2008, three months to the day of my wife's passing, I attended a workshop on therapeutic touch. This came about as a friend asked me if I would like to attend a conference with her as she thought this may be of interest to me. The guest speaker was a woman unfamiliar to me by the name of Christine Page. I agreed to go and when we arrived at the conference centre, to my surprise, I was one of only 5 men in a room of approximately 300 women. I realized much of the material presented in this workshop was already known to me as a result of what I witnessed and experienced during my wife's cancer journey. There was a book signing at the end of the presentation and my friend wanted to have her book signed by Christine Page. We quickly made our way to the front of the line and I told my friend that since I didn't have any questions for Christine, I would just stand off to the side and wait as my friend had her book signed.

What happened next was quite unexpected and remarkable. As Christine was signing my friend's book she looked toward me and asked me, as one of the few men in the audience, what I thought of the presentation. I told her that a lot of what was presented was already familiar to me because of what I experienced during my wife's cancer journey, but that I did enjoy learning about the chakras. I then told Christine that what I also got out of her workshop was confirmation as to some of the spiritual messages that I received from my wife. Christine asked me if I was writing, and I said that I did some writing while my wife was in the palliative unit, she then asked me if I had put those writings into a book; I responded by telling her that I had not as of yet. I went on to tell Christine that it was interesting that she asked me that question, because it happened to be one of the spiritual messages that my wife had given me before she passed; my wife asked me to write a book. Christine smiled and said, "I know silly, she is telling me to tell you again." Christine then told me that I was unusual and so out of curiosity I replied, "Why would you say that I am unusual?" Christine answered me by saying, "Being a male having had your experience and by what you know today, you are like me." I then said, "But I don't think you're unusual." Christine said, "You don't, because we understand each other, but trust me, I am considered unusual." Pointing to one of the conference rooms, Christine said, "You should be out there and I look forward to reading your book and hearing you speak one day." The conference room that Christine pointed to just so happened to be room number eleven.

My friend, with a look of amazement turned toward me and she asked me to ask Christine if there were any more messages. So, I asked Christine if she had any more messages for me from my wife. Christine told me that she did and picked up a large size book with both hands raised above her head, in a motion as if to hit me over the head and said, "Get on with it!" My friend, who knew my wife very well said, "That's her, that's something she would say!" I had to agree, it's true, that is something my wife would say to me in that manner.

Looking back now, this experience was more profound than it appeared to be at the time, and it has more significance and meaning to me than it did then. At the time, it was surreal to say the least, but not something that I deeply pondered as I continued on with my life. It was only as I was completing this book and seriously considering speaking publicly that I realized that this particular experience was more than an unexplained, psychic coincidence. I suppose that there were many things that happened since the passing of my wife that seemed surreal at the time, but somehow became more significant and profound to me as my journey continued to where I am today.

Meeting Christine Page helped to validate the spiritual messages I received from my wife, and as a result, reinforced within me the importance of believing and accepting my experience and the path that has been laid before me.

Prayer Wheel Program

The prayer wheel was developed by Dr. John Rossiter-Thornton as a self-help tool that can be used by anyone, no matter what his background or beliefs. The wheel consists of eight components, and although five minutes are recommended for each, you can shorten or remove segments according to your preference. Dr. Rossiter-Thornton recommends that even if you shorten some of the steps you should keep a full five minutes for the "listen" segment. Proceeding clockwise from the top of the wheel, the steps of the prayer wheel as recommended by Dr. Rossiter-Thornton are as follows:

1. "Count your blessings" and give thanks and praise. Reflect on the things for which you are thankful.

2. Sing of love. Choose and sing a favorite love song.

3. Request protection and guidance. Ask for protection and guidance for you and your loved ones.

4. Forgive yourself and others.

5. Ask for needs, yours and others. Record and date your requests for anything you or your loved ones need.

6. "Fill me with love" and inspirations. Think about the things that make you feel hope, love, and inspiration.

7. LISTEN with pen (and paper) in hand. The most important step, listening involves sitting quietly while being receptive to any thoughts, images, feelings, words, or ideas. Write down whatever comes to mind.

8. "Your will is my will." Put yourself in the hands of your higher power and trust that it has your best interests at heart.

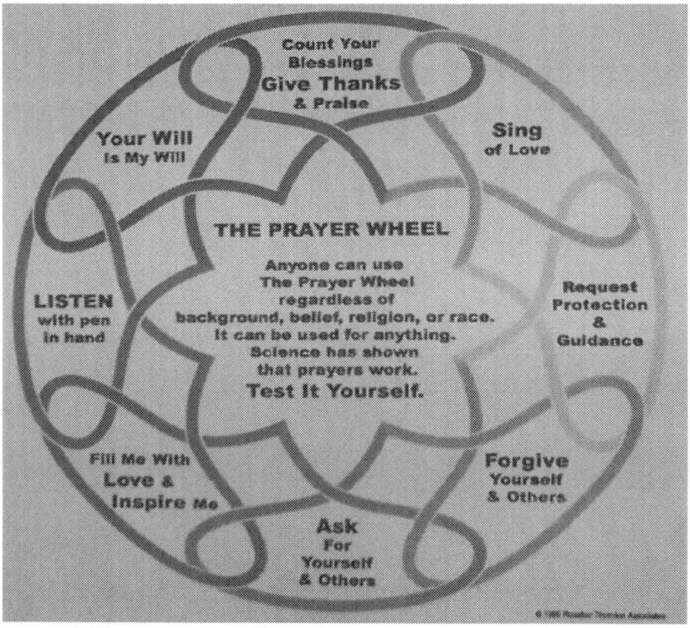

If it was not for the encouragement and guidance of Dr. Thornton, I would not have written a single flow. On many occasions when I had questions or concerns in my life Dr. Thornton would urge me to do a flow. Several flows in this book are a direct result of Dr. Thornton challenging me to write a flow in response to a question or situation. I would leave his office with a sense of trepidation every time he would ask me to do a flow. I would then return the following week with flow in hand and would read it to him. I expected to hear a diplomatic negative response. I asked Dr. Thornton if he really thought the flows were good and if they made sense to him and to my surprise Dr. Thornton saw value in them.

The Prayer Wheel Flows are best read slowly while pausing between sentences; I like to refer to this as "meditative reading."

"Skepticism can be a healthy approach to learning when balanced with an *open mind*."

Reference; Rossiter-Thornton Enterprises Inc. P.O. Box 804 Postal Station Q Toronto, Ontario. Canada M4T 2P4. www.theprayerwheel.com

My Spiritual Awakening

My wife's cancer journey was a sad journey of suffering, but one that proved to be a journey of discovery and hope in the end. This is what I would like people to realize and understand as they read this book. The message that I'd like people to take from reading this book is that fear is our greatest enemy and that we are life and life does not know death. Knowing this truth deep down in your heart will change the way you face the challenges of life.

The message may not be unfamiliar to some, but the profundity of this message lies within the spiritual experiences and the scientifically unexplained events that were captured in this book. These events should be discerned in a manner that causes self-reflection and introspection; a silent pause to deeply contemplate and meditate on its validity and its significance in supporting a spiritual philosophy.

As I questioned the long journey of my wife's cancer, I realized that her battle to stay alive was a journey of self-discovery as well. This journey of self-discovery was in part, as a result of trying to make sense of all that was happening to us; why me, life isn't fair, why would a loving god allow a good person to suffer when there are those who harm and still prosper? This became a search for truth and the truth needed to make sense. This was a search for healing that took us to places and before people that we would not have known or sought out.

On one hand my wife's fear of dying was her imprisonment, while on the other hand it was the motivational means to unlocking my spiritual self. Before my wife's cancer journey, I had little reason to question who I was or why I was here. Like most, I did not question being born into a pre-existing operational world that arguably was, and still is, dysfunctional. I blindly accepted the educational model that was provided for me; I was forced to embrace a religion that by all accounts was said to be the best of its kind; I had to make money to survive and earn a living, and I had to figure out for myself how to set boundaries and nurture relationships as I matured. Even though I did not truly understand the vast world that surrounded me or who I truly was; I was able to reach adulthood relatively unscathed.

My wife's fear, courage and will to live taught me a lot about myself. I learned the principles of compassion, dignity, courage, and integrity. As a result of having exercised these principles on a daily basis, I was able to open my heart further to reveal my deeper self; my true spiritual self.

To become aware of your spiritual identity is a powerful thing; you no longer have to go through life wondering why. By knowing your true identity you begin to trust yourself and in turn gain knowledge to take control of your life by using the tools of love and accountability. In knowing your true identity and by being true to yourself, you become aligned with the power of good. In knowing your true identity and by being true to yourself, you receive a higher wisdom and knowledge of love that allows you to control and overcome fear. In knowing your true identity and by being true to yourself, you surround yourself with a certain kind of peace and security that can only be derived from the courage of the heart.

The title of my book, "Unlocking My Spiritual Self" is not intended to be interpreted as being religious in nature or as a religious statement; rather, it is a personal statement of awakening and the result of choosing love and compassion over money, which put me on a path of inner discovery. I had to choose between the fear that was in my mind and the courage that was within my heart; the fear of walking away from my business and the courage to commit unconditionally and serve my wife during her pain and suffering.

This was a frightening prospect for me, I had no idea how we would survive financially. Throwing caution to the wind, I listened to my conscience and followed my heart; I became a caregiver and was no longer a business man. I was challenged in ways that were equally as challenging if not more challenging than running a business. I was challenged to see beyond the suffering, the anger, the criticism, and the blame that accompany pain and suffering in order to serve my wife unconditionally. I could not do this without continually increasing a connection to my heart, which meant continually putting my daily personal needs aside to focus only on the needs of my wife. Putting this into practice on a daily basis sounds easier than it is, especially over a prolonged period of time and under very trying circumstances. I believe what made this easier for me was witnessing the heart breaking look of fear in my wife's eyes and knowing that she could not deal with the thought of dying from cancer. I felt more like a protective parent caring for his child than a husband having to put his needs aside. There was no walking away from this situation for me; I knew I was going to see this through to the end, whatever the end would be. I had no idea that committing to the care of my wife would lead to an awakening of truth and unlocking my spiritual self.

I had many reservations in writing about the spiritual experiences I encountered on this journey. I knew that many would not easily accept these experiences to be true. I knew that if I were to read about these experiences, I too would have my doubts. It's not easy to believe in such things unless you have had the same personal experience to draw from. Eventually, I came to the realization that I have no control over what others believe to be truth. All I can do is tell my story with the hope that this will be an opportunity for the reader to go beyond their present frame of reference to question what their reasoning mind wants to reject. Sharing my experience and story is part of my continued service to others in order to awaken them to unlocking their spiritual self. My wife`s eleven year cancer journey put me into a school of learning like no other. I learned so much through this experience which has been made known through the sampling of my Prayer Wheel Flows within this book. I learned things about life and myself that I would not have ever of known if it were not for my wife's cancer. I learned about the power of good, love, and of the power of accountability. We have heard about mind over matter; which is a useful tool to assist us in life. I learned about another more powerful tool that knows no boundaries called soul over matter. Soul over matter uses the inner wisdom within the conscience of the heart. Listening to our conscience, trusting our conscience, and understanding our conscience elevates mind over matter to unite it with the power of soul over matter.

Soul over matter is about thinking with the heart or consciousness and not with the mind or ego. I came to the realization that we are not our circumstances but rather, we are the source of the lessons within those circumstances. This realization meant that I had to accept my circumstances with love and courage and not deny them through anger or fear. I became aware that I had freewill and the choice to take control of my circumstances or be controlled by them. I recognized that when I was being controlled by my circumstances, I was under the control of my ego by way of fear and anxiety. Surrendering to my circumstance and accepting the fact that "it is what it is," with the knowing that I was a good person was all I had left in my situation. My surrendering to my circumstance, by letting go of the outcome, turned out to be an important first step toward humbling me to the higher power of good within me. I slowly began letting go of my mind by surrendering it to my heart with a "do and don't think" approach to my circumstances. This simple humbling philosophy means exactly what it states; just do whatever you have to do in your circumstance and don't think about the outcome. In using this "last resort" philosophy, I was unaware at the time that I was actually taking the first steps toward uncovering my power within and the power of love. I was unaware that I was about to uncover an inner wisdom with unlimited possibilities just waiting to serve me. Truth and knowledge that had been dormant within me was about to be realized for the first time, and this thirst and hunger for truth and knowledge that we all have within us was about to be quenched.

The "do and don't think" approach opened the door to many teachings. It taught me that I had to live a day at a time in order to endure my circumstances. It taught me to have courage by trusting the unknown, it taught me that I had to take responsibility and be accountable for my life circumstance. It taught me that by trusting and believing in myself, I would come to know the "I am" within me. It also taught me to face my fears with the inner power of love. Finally, it taught me that the power of love is not realized without courage and accountability.

The cancer journey of my wife coupled with the guidance and encouragement I received from Dr. Thornton, as well as, by using the Prayer Wheel techniques, led to this book being written. I don`t consider myself a writer. This art of flowing is simple and available to all who wish to learn. To flow is to connect and become one with your experience and to open yourself up to your heart through meditation or quiet time. Flowing is the art of listening to your inner voice to receive guidance from within. Ask a question and then wait until a word or thought "pops" into your mind. Then chase this word or thought with another question. Repeat this process and a picture will eventually begin to unfold. Don't judge what comes, remove fear and allow yourself to get lost within this process. One flow will eventually become part of the next flow and the next flow will also add to the previous flow. The invisible creates the visible; there is great wisdom to be uncovered within every person who dares to look within.

Unlocking your spiritual self involves expanding your mind and heart. It's not enough to just awaken to your heart. Your heart has to take control of your mind. Your mind has to trust your heart and become one with your heart; this allows for your inner wisdom to be transmitted to you. Step outside the box of your mind's eye and do not be trapped by past thoughts.

You know you have unlocked your spiritual self when:

You recognize your conscience as a fountain of wisdom within your heart.

You reason and lead with your heart and not your mind.

You are able to see truth beyond the illusion of the physical body.

You are able to see truth beyond the illusion of death.

You are accountable to your life experience.

You take responsibility for your life experience.

You recognize that all life lessons are lessons of love.

You are consciously aware of the need to strive to overcome self.

You realize fear is your worst enemy in life.

You recognize and understand that you are here to serve the greater good of mankind.

Your experience in this life time is uniquely yours and you need to accept and embrace it with a spiritual knowledge of your true self. Being true to yourself will help to align you with your true purpose in life and overcome the lessons that are uniquely yours.

Changing yourself to align with your true self is one of the biggest challenges you can ever undertake, but it is the most rewarding journey that you can derive the greatest and most fulfilling benefits from. Have the courage to make a connection to your heart and overcome any fear that is preventing you to seek your truth within. You are a creator as your creator is within you and your possibilities are therefore endless.

Prayer Wheel Flows

'Whispered Words of Wisdom'

Prayer Wheel Flow
On
Team Spirit Within

Unleash the shackles of the mind and set yourself free. Man was given a mind to think and a heart to counsel. There must be unity, harmony, and a team spirit within if man is to develop and progress. For if one is of the mind more than of the heart, then one is more apt to take advantage of others, and if one is of the heart more than of the mind, then one is more apt to be taken advantage of. Both are the result of a manipulated and swayed ego. Imagine living in a world where man has a mind but no heart; imagine living in a world where man has a heart but no mind. There can be no peace or harmony in such a world of extreme bias. One should make every effort and strive to achieve balance between mind and heart. The aim of the mind should be to consult the heart and the aim of the heart should be to enlighten and direct the mind. Disharmony within and disharmony without are reflections of an inner team discord, conflict, and struggle. The mind and the heart are coexisting inharmoniously. The selfish ego feels endangered and vulnerable by the selfless heart, for the temporary nature of things has captivated the ego and entrapped it within the fear of the mind. Through experiences the ego is given opportunities to awaken and receive the truth within the heart. This is to say, with each experience there is encouragement and assistance provided to awaken the mind to recognize and allow the wisdom of the heart. For the mind and heart need to coexist harmoniously as a requirement and prerequisite of unconditional service. For it is this team spirit within that will set man free and allow man to co create peace on earth.

T.S. December 13, 2010

Prayer Wheel Flow
On
Soul Persuasion

For this being a world of illusion, one may think there are countless decisions, choices, and options which in some way unite to create a significant self-transformation. The reality is, there are only a small number of decisions, choices, and options that are offered within any given lifetime which contribute in any significant way to ones self-transformation. For when we speak of a significant self-transformation experience, we are speaking of a deep heartfelt and profound make over having taken place within ones heart and mind. This is a required makeover, having been orchestrated by the soul to better serve others. For the soul speaks with the camouflaged language of love, for the soul speaks with a hidden style of purpose, and the soul is focused on overcoming and rising above the outer self. The persuasion of the soul wills itself through predestined life experiences. The persuasion of the soul's purpose is to simultaneously sway and dissuade thoughts and actions within these predestined life experiences. Think of having the experience of being safe and sound in a room and then having the lights slowly dimmed to pitch black. Now the only safe haven available is the small light visible under a doorway from beyond. This dilemma forms the opportunity for change. This is a crisis created to sway you to move toward the light beyond the room, as well as, dissuade you from living in a room of darkness. Now the choice is yours, it always has been. The more connected you are to your heart, the less fear you will have moving from darkness to light and toward the persuasion of your soul. The less connected you are to your heart, the more fear you will have moving toward this light. For it is the love within the heart that invites and accepts the light, while it is the fear of the mind that resists and mistrusts the light, and as a result, continues to live in darkness. Therefore, do not fear love, but rather, be afraid of fear itself. For now is the time to become aware, now is the time to awaken to the way of your heart and the perspective and persuasion of your soul.

T.S. July 16, 2010

Prayer Wheel Flow
On
Spiritual Improvising

Is my life experience meant to serve me? The answer may seem obvious to most. For a simple yes does not explain how; the how depends on whether you accept or deny your experience. Acceptance of your experience allows you to create in the now, while denial of your experience prevents you from being creative. Acceptance of your experience allows you to truly discover yourself; while denial of your experience blocks you from truly understanding yourself. Acceptance of your experience allows you to carry on and endure, while denial of your experience creates doubt and brings you to a halt. For the type of experience we speak of is not superficial in nature or skin deep, but one which penetrates deep within the heart and mind. Such an experience wears the mask or guise of an accident, misfortune, or bad luck. In actual fact, a profound experience in most cases has been pre-planned, predestined, and known by you. For this is a spiritual play in which the characters, plots, scenes, challenges, and circumstances have been created by you. This is to experience and understand the real you, the little god within you, for the purpose of co-creation. You are all actors improvising as you go; for the freedom to improvise within the limits of any given scene or experience created by you is the only freewill you really have. Improvising within freewill decides the outcome and progression made toward or away from the knowledge and wisdom of that experience. Improvising to optimize your freewill choices within any given scene or experience depends on your ability to take direction. Spiritual improvising is paying attention to instinct, intuition, and common sense. Spiritual improvising is a matter of trust and having confidence in this inner wisdom which is an aspect of the true self. If you cannot trust your true inner self to guide and direct your performances who then can you trust? Spiritual improvising is taking what has been gained thus far from experience and turning it into an instrument of co-creation.

T.S. May 15, 2010

Prayer Wheel Flow
On
Seeing Beyond Your Physical Body

How does one explain a knowing, how does one justify and describe having inner wisdom and how does one awaken to see through things? For the darkness of the night conceals and obscures the exactness and truth of the lighted day, for the darkness of the night manipulates and confuses the senses and intelligence of the lighted day and the darkness of the night gives rise to fear not apparent or noticeable in the light of the day. For if one was to journey from day to night, illumination to darkness surrendering to the manipulation and confusion of the night; would not fear take hold, befriend and imprison them to illusion and deception. For the truth of the light and wisdom of the day would have to be retrieved and revealed to provide the peace and strength of character necessary to stay and endure the darkness of the night. For the light is an aspect of the spiritual realm and the dark an aspect of the physical realm. For you come from the light of the spiritual realm to experience the darkness of the physical realm, while in the physical realm you are always connected to the light through a knowing, an inner wisdom and a sense from within. This light within is turned on and further awakened by accepting and enduring a prolonged and purposeful challenging experience. A prolonged and purposeful challenging experience always contains within it the opportunity to awaken you to the real you, the spiritual you and to your true inner self. Thy Kingdom come, Thy will be done, on earth as it is in heaven means connecting, uniting and harmonizing man's individual innocent heart to gods unconditional loving heart. For when one enters into partnership with divine, one becomes the means of access for the spirit and the light of endless love to flow through. For the intention of this light is to serve the physical world by illuminating and transforming all darkness in its path. For the Kingdom of heaven is on its way and will have its day as man continues opening his heart further to see beyond the physical body.

T.S. November 20, 2009

Prayer Wheel Flow
On
Eleven, Eleven

You are being ruled by the energy of 11:11; for this is a space in time intended to liberate and unshackle, for this is an opportunity to attain closure and create anew. All lessons have a cause and effect and must be answered in time. This depends on the consciousness of the soul. This awareness and awakening takes place as a result of soul standing. The soul standing of one is representative of their cumulative commitment to truth. One's present day attributes, abilities, and qualities reveal this genuine commitment. All lessons are individual, uniquely different, and yet all lessons support the same purpose. The purpose is to serve and without accountability the level of service will remain under the control of the ego. Being accountable to your past, present and future self will increase the ability to better serve others and the universe as a whole. There are reasons for everything that happens and accountability provides a sense of balance needed to appreciate and work out those reasons. Therefore, balance occurs as a result of knowledge and wisdom gained through the experience of accountability. Without accountability truth remains but a mystery and service unimportant. To repeatedly see this number eleven is a sign one has come to the teaching space of service through the doorway of accountability. The energy of 11:11 provides guidance and protection needed from working against self. Overcoming self is the pathway toward accountability, truth, and service.

"One of the most difficult things is not to change society -but to change yourself." ~Nelson Mandela

T.S. May 20, 2011

Prayer Wheel Flow
On
To Turn the Other Cheek

What does it mean to "turn the other cheek?" What is the significance of "turning the other cheek?" What are the lessons to be learned from turning the other cheek? For the purpose of a physical life on earth is to learn about who we are. We are here to learn about our true potential to co-create; the mechanics, inner workings, and the accountability associated with co-creation. For we have unique features, attributes, and abilities that allow us to create, which includes our ability to think, feel, perceive, act and react as a result of our freewill. We need to understand how we create all things that we perceive as good and all things that we perceive as bad. To express or orchestrate actions or reactions involves using your creative system, whether you do this spontaneously or whether you do this exercising great care. For if you have hate within your heart, realize you created this with your creative system and tools of creation. Thoughts and emotions is magnetic energy and this energy has attracted hate in the form of events or experiences. Likewise, if you have love within your heart, realize you created this with your creative system and tools of creation. Recognizing this to be true, you will then know and understand that one who slaps the face of another slaps himself in return. Therefore, revenge is pure ignorance as a result of not understanding the inner workings of one's creative powers. Therefore, do not engage in retaliation, for this will only create a negative karmic cycle. A karmic cycle binds and locks you into a merry go round of like experiences. You are able to free yourself by being accountable and taking responsibility for your life circumstances; this is a required prerequisite for co-creation. There is also an aspect of forgiveness which is an important lesson in humility. Humility is essential as part of understanding co-creation. To understand the true meaning and significance behind "turn the other cheek" is to understand the power of forgiveness and how this relates to the purpose of life on earth.

T.S. January 20, 2010

Prayer Wheel Flow
On
Spiritual Calling

There is no sense of duty or obligation to a spiritual calling; a spiritual calling is an invitation and a spiritual calling is a carefully selected opportunity relevant to you. A spiritual calling offers a passage of possibility to seek out the true identity of self. Truth resides within every challenge, for where life offers a challenge it also offers opportunity. A spiritual calling is an opportunity to express gratitude and show appreciation for the challenge. For without a challenge there is ignorance and a lack of responsibility and without a challenge there is indifference and egotism. A spiritual calling is a challenge, for it is not the pinnacle of life as some would like to believe. With all challenges there is a responsibility to overcome, and a spiritual calling is no different. Everything in life is earned one way or another. When faced with a spiritual calling you have freewill, therefore there are no exact or inexact responses. Your past freewill decisions and choices have reaped you a spiritual harvest. Deny this fruit of labour today and look back tomorrow with a sense of uncertainty, doubt, and void. Accept this fruit of labour and move toward a higher purpose of service with faith and certainty. Your present choices will influence and impact your awaiting spiritual path. You may run until you are weary, but you cannot hide from a soothing, gentle, and compassionate light of a spiritual calling.

T.S. April 14, 2011

Prayer Wheel Flow
On
Spiritual Oxygen

The human body can go without water for weeks, the human body can go without food for months, but the human body can only go without oxygen for a mere moment. Oxygen is a vital and essential source of physical life. In the spiritual sense oxygen is love. Oxygen is like an endless well of love to nourish all life. Oxygen is to the physical world what love is to the spiritual world. For both are invisible energies that become quite visible when put to use, for both are invisible energies which support and assist in the physical experience, as well as, in the spiritual existence. Both oxygen and love must maintain a healthy balance to serve unconditionally. For the intelligence of the body instinctively and intuitively knows to draw in and breathe out oxygen to maintain optimum health. However, the intelligence of the heart has been ignored and overlooked, thus, creating an imbalance between giving and receiving. As a result of these imbalances, countless lessons of love have shaped man's experience. For if the true essence of man is physical and material in nature, then despite the consequences of experience and not withstanding an accident; food, water, and oxygen should be sufficient to maintain and sustain optimal health. The truth is when love is absent, suppressed, or withheld from life; food, water and oxygen is not enough to maintain and sustain optimal health. For love is a life giving blanket of air, spiritual in nature, surrounding and supporting the earth, accessible only through a connection to the heart. This connection is similar to putting on a spiritual oxygen mask; wherein the heart acts as a channel and a means for spiritual oxygen to flow through and bring into materialization a sense of peace, wellbeing, and optimum health. For there will always be pain and suffering, greed and illness, war and violence in the physical world, as long as man mistakenly sees himself as a physical being first. The truth exists; for man remains a spiritual being partaking in a temporary physical experience. As such, to facilitate and maintain optimum health, man must trust and not ignore the intelligence within his heart. This will enable man to connect to a life giving and spiritual source of oxygen called love.

Prayer Wheel Flow
On
Reaching Out

Going beyond self to reach out and help another is like diving into the uncertainty of deep waters. Diving into deep water requires courage, ability, and faith. Without love and compassion, one may take the plunge, but the entry will be that of an adolescent. Reaching out requires a level of maturity; maturity and age do not always march together. One may be young and mature and one may be old but lacking maturity. The maturity of love and compassion will oversee the service of reaching out. For one cannot truly nurture, support, or comfort another without it. Reaching out requires the maturity of truth, for truth is an honest heart to heart communication. Truth penetrates deeper through the heart than through the mind, for the mind will follow the truth of the heart. Reaching out requires the maturity of having mindfulness of the heart, mindfulness of the heart means being aware of the heart in the present moment. This conscious awareness is essential to realize and recognize the pain, sorrow, and heartache of another. Only through this awareness and perspective of pain can one connect to their true inner self. Objectivity and selflessness reside within the true inner self. Reaching out without objectivity and selflessness is a vain display, for there will be distortions or bias to simply serve the adolescent ego. The attribute of the true self is selflessness which consists of three pillars. The first pillar is unconditional love, the second pillar is unconditional service, and the third pillar is unconditional forgiveness. The three pillars of selflessness in turn support one's own peace and harmony. Therefore one's own peace and harmony support humanity and the universal oneness through the act of reaching out to another.

T.S. April 18, 2011

Prayer Wheel Flow
On
Purpose

For one's life purpose is not always served to them on a platter. For one's spiritual reasons, objectives, and goals are usually realized and masked within their earned abilities. Earned abilities are meant to serve others; for these are gifts earned through experience. Your experiences help to awaken you to recognize your spiritual abilities. For if you were born into wealth and were provided with the means to become a doctor, would this mean your purpose in life is to be a doctor? The answer may possibly be yes, but the question one ought to ask to discover their real purpose is, what sort of a doctor? What approach, attitude, and means would best serve others? The experience of becoming a doctor represents a small fraction or part of the overall purpose. To awaken to see beyond procedural, technical, and mechanical routines represents the deeper understanding and meaning relevant to their purpose. This is to say, within any given field of study or situation in life, your earned abilities are shaped by how you respond and react to the challenges connected to that experience. Within that experience there are usually lessons and understanding needed to find closure to a past life circumstance. The manner in which this is done affects your potential to create anew and thus recognize your inherent, natural, spiritual abilities to better serve others. Finding closure while creating a new takes place simultaneously; this serves with the intention to stimulate and awaken you to discover your spiritual identity. Therefore, one should ask what my abilities are and what my strengths are. Within those questions lie the answers to discovering your rightful purpose. Within those questions is where the realization of your true self will emerge. Remember, this is a search within your heart, to make use of, and utilize your earned spiritual abilities. There is a reason, a cause, and an effect for everything that happens. Therefore, there is a purpose for everything that happens. Nothing happens without service. Therefore, it is service which governs purpose to sustain and nourish all life.

T.S. May 27, 2010

Prayer Wheel Flow
On
Psalm 23

What is the meaning, significance and wisdom of Psalm 23? For Psalm 23 expresses unconditional love and absolute faith, Psalm 23 communicates accountability and responsibility. Psalm 23 seeks to awaken the logical mind to unite and connect to the intelligence and wisdom within the loving heart. For when we say the Lord is my Shepherd I shall not want, we are saying, for the Lord is thy law and thy law is love. The universe is governed by love, and out of love arises wisdom, this wisdom in turn serves as the governing law of love. For love and wisdom within the heart heals and guides, for this love within the heart empowers. This allows one to rest and smell the flowers when walking along a challenging course and spiritual path toward infinite knowledge. This love within empowers, it takes one to a stream of calm and peace within when walking along the difficult course toward infinite truth. This is a physical world of illusion capable of creating delusion, shepherding man toward ignorance and fear, and influencing freewill. A valley is capable of casting a temporary dark shadow upon the surface of the earth. This shadow demonstrates how darkness can exist within light, yet the shadow or darkness is just a physical illusion; for if it were real it would be permanent and last forever. Death is the shadow of life and evil is the shadow of love, for both death and evil are the effects of a cause. The cause is ignorance and fear, created by delusion, as a consequence and result of illusion. It is said; by means of a Shepherd's rod and staff one shall not fear and shall find comfort. For one is saying, by means of love and wisdom within the heart, one shall find guidance and protection needed to overcome fear and be comforted. To prepare a table in the presence of my enemy means to offer love in the presence of darkness, to illuminate, enlighten, and serve through forgiveness. For it is through your level of love and service toward others which protects and guides; it is through your level of love and service toward others that allows ascension beyond this physical world of illusion; this, to forever dwell in the higher frequencies and vibrations of infinite love.

T.S. October 16, 2009

Prayer Wheel Flow
On
Placebo Effect

If you have no doubts ask and you shall receive the answer you seek. If you have no suspicions seek and you shall find the solution you desire, for this is the cause and effect of real faith. Faith is but an empty screen, faith is sightless and blind. Faith is ineffective without the essence of knowledge, wisdom, and understanding. For when we speak of a placebo effect, we are speaking of a desired result achieved through the artificial creation of real faith. For a placebo in the form of a pill is an example of this, it has the essence of knowledge, wisdom, and understanding within it to remove all doubt and suspicion. A placebo is a means to a positive end by removing all negating factors, a placebo is a means to creating a positive result by removing nullifying effects, and a placebo is a means to achieve real faith by removing self-sabotaging behaviour. Realize all results are influenced through a combination of these varying levels of doubt and certainties. For a placebo in pill form removes all level of doubt in order to allow for a level of absolute certainty or real faith to exist. For a placebo to be effective there cannot be contradiction; likewise, for the law of attraction to be effective, there can be no contradiction. One cannot expect good to manifest while thinking and feeling ill about those things. Therefore, to create a placebo type effect, one must first reconcile with everything in the universe, for when you are so reconciled and grateful, only good can come. For this power of good is the only power which truly exists in life, everything else is delusion. This is the only true power which creates and sustains all life, and this is the only true power which removes all doubt and suspicion. Therefore, a universe perceived to be good will produce results similar to that of a placebo effect. A placebo effect in pill form is further proof that coincidences or accidents do not truly exist. They are the effects of the cause created and attracted by way of thoughts, perceptions, emotions, and actions. A placebo effect in pill form is a perfect scientific model to enlighten man to the mechanisms, systems, and inner workings of real faith and the great spiritual law of attraction.

T.S. February 1, 2010

Prayer Wheel Flow
On
My Energy

When we speak of my energy, we are speaking of creative energy, a source of intention, a foundation of purpose, and we are speaking of the cause of all effect. This is a conscious force which knowingly flows throughout the universe and permeates all living things. For ones thoughts, emotions, and actions are a means and channel to transport, direct and guide these creative energies. For this is done by way of frequencies and vibrations. When one has a thought, be it good, bad, or indifferent, that thought has an inherent, creative frequency and vibration assigned to it. High frequency thoughts and emotions will trigger and produce higher vibrations. Low frequency thoughts and emotions will trigger and produce lower vibrations. The higher the vibration the brighter the light, the brighter the light the more resourceful and creative the energy will be. You are creative energy, residing within creative energy, surrounded by creative energy and forever connected to creative energy. For you serve energy and energy serves you. A profound physical experience is designed to stimulate, influence, and manipulate these energies by way of one's discernment and perception. A profound physical experience is designed to bring forth change and transformation, thus demanding and consuming a vast amount of energy both physically and mentally. A profound physical experience is then followed by a metamorphic stage. This is a time of letting go, a time of renewal, and a time of restoring ones energy. For this is a priceless and meaningful time and a therapeutic step to develop and grow in acceptance. Acceptance of the heart is essential to benefit from a profound physical experience. Acceptance of the heart brings forth a sense of peace to connect us to a higher vibration of creative energy and love. How else can one reap the benefits of change to better serve self and others?

April 15, 2010

Prayer Wheel Flow
On
Learning Lessons of Love in a World of Duality

Suffering awakens the soul, misfortune elevates the spirit, and adversity develops ones strength of character. For in a physical world of duality and contradiction, like attracts like and opposites attract. For in a physical world of duality and contradiction two different and opposing suggestions, outcomes or conclusions create the logical. For one awakens to learn the lessons of love through suffering, misfortune and adversity. One has the power to attract, create, and manifest love by means of one's emotions, thoughts and by means of one's enduring pursuit of love. You must first seek to understand, appreciate and value that which you want to create before you can realize its fruitfulness. For an intention which lacks knowledge and understanding will attract the lessons of that intention in the form of a contradiction. Contradiction is designed to awaken the conscious mind to the inner being, to further understand, appreciate, and value that which it seeks. As you are a child of your past and the parent of your future, you are constantly finding closure to past mistakes while simultaneously creating anew. You are habitually, without thought, seeking to find unconditional love within yourself and in others. Learning to love another unconditionally in a world of duality involves acquiring knowledge in order to see the spiritual nature within them. Learning to love another unconditionally in a world of duality involves acquiring the knowledge in order to appreciate and accept the uniqueness within them. Learning to love another unconditionally in a world of duality involves acquiring knowledge in order to recognize the true self within them. Only through a physical experience can you learn to understand yourself to then understand others. Only through a physical experience can you learn to appreciate yourself to then appreciate others, and only through a physical experience can you learn to value yourself to then value others. Therefore, seek to connect to the inner wisdom of your heart, for there you will find your protection, guidance, and the knowledge needed to better understand and appreciate the lessons of love in a meaningful way.

T.S. December 7, 2009

Prayer Wheel Flow
On
Heavenly Love

Heavenly love exists within every heart and waits patiently to be awakened. A love which strives to prove itself contradicts the true inner self and serves the outer ego; a love which seeks to be noticed is never above the suspicion of man. The outward manifestation of heavenly love is beautiful and beauty needs no makeup to be known. For all those who support and favor the practice of selling love must realize they are merely substituting heavenly love with manmade love. Manmade love is a love backed by authority and accepted to be true and trusted as the best of its kind. Heavenly love is angelic; for it is blameless, without guilt, and without sin, for it is kind, beautiful and sweet. Heavenly love has the appearance and expression of an innocent child. It has been said that only a child is ready for the kingdom of heaven. For I say, one must think as an adult but remain as a child to access the inner wisdom of the heart and enter into the kingdom of Heavenly Love. The only barrier and struggle standing between man and his heart is his ego. The ego, seeking to protect the innocent child within has inadvertently denied and cut off access to the wisdom of the heart. One should be open, naïve, and without suspicion when it comes to allowing and listening to the wisdom of their heart. For all that is good originates within the heart of man. Everything in your life is an experience that awakens and connects you to the inner wisdom of your heart. Everything in your life is nudging you to realize your true self and everything in your life acts as a blueprint toward Heavenly Love.

T.S. April 4, 2011

Prayer Wheel Flow
On
Awaken and Serve Truth

Awaken my child, come to life; for one should not have to live in denial and one should not have to live in disharmony. Allow truth to serve you and allow yourself to serve truth. For you have come to truth and truth has come to you, accept this reality. Realize, in the end, it is truth which generates all experience and it is experience which validates all truth. Come out of yourself and serve in this light of truth. Connect to the undercurrent of truth which flows beneath all experiences and which flows beneath your own personal experiences. For beneath the surface of each experience exists the wisdom and intelligence of love. This wisdom and intelligence of love becomes visible as service and is the undercurrent of truth which flows beneath all experiences. Rise up to this challenge, awaken to serve truth. If you choose not to at this time, understand truth will not stop serving you, for truth is love. For this choice to awaken and serve truth is yours, it always has been, choose wisely.

T.S. December 6, 2010

Prayer Wheel Flow
On
Spirit Soul Evolution

All difficulties and obstacles are tests and trials of the spirit. How else can a spirit come to realize its infinite power and possibilities and how else can a spirit come to appreciate the light? For you cannot have dark without light and you cannot have light without dark; you cannot have shadow without sunshine and you cannot have sunshine without shadow. One cannot exist without the other, for they are two parts which make up the whole and they are two parts that serve each other. The darkness of pain and suffering is not the wrath of god, the darkness of pain and suffering is not a form of punishment. For the darkness of pain and suffering is a result of the law of cause and effect. This has its rewards and compensations which guide us toward the light of enlightenment. For pain and suffering has been misjudged, for that which belongs to the eternal evolution of an infinite spirit soul's journey cannot be understood from a transient, physical perspective. The physical eyes of matter are clouded by the transient and temporary nature of things. For truth can only be appreciated and understood through the eyes of the eternal spirit and soul. To overcome your difficulties, to conquer your handicaps, and to triumph over your pain and suffering has its rewards and compensation. It can awaken you to your spirit and to your soul and thus quicken its evolution. From a spiritual perspective there is no greater reward or compensation than this. The spirit cannot grow and evolve without challenges and obstacles. Can ones spirit grow and evolve if every difficulty was removed and taken care of? If there was nothing to conquer, there would be no growth or evolution of spirit and there would be no purpose of being. This physical world provides the best learning experience to evolve. Embrace this spiritual wisdom, and when you find yourself on a path of pain and suffering, know this is your opportunity to awaken to your spirit and soul. This is your destiny to awaken and your classroom to discover the power and possibilities of your spirit and soul. This is an essential and valuable part of your spirit soul's evolution.

T.S. January 13, 2009

Prayer Wheel Flow
On
World of Judgement

Can man be taught through religious compromise, can man find truth through religious concessions, and can man gain knowledge through religious conformities? Religious convictions are rooted in fear, ignorance and idealism. For the physical world has been dominated and controlled through the masculine intellectual mind. This masculine domination has led to an invitation which has allowed for the dark forces weapon of choice and path of fear to reign supreme on planet earth. As a result this has over shadowed the feminine and emotional feeling heart, whose guidance and path is toward unconditional love. As a result of this imbalance, man has created a world built upon fear and the off-spring of fear which is judgement. For a world based on judgement has the capability and means of casting out an ambiguous shadow of compromise, concessions, and conformities, which are evident in the manufacturing and creation of various religions which dominate this physical world. For if fear and judgement did not exist in this physical world nor would religion exist in this physical world. Judgement is the consequence of a manipulated mind, and a manipulated mind is the consequence of implanted thoughts of fear. Implanted thoughts of fear are the consequence of ignorance, and ignorance is the consequence and result of illusion. Illusion is created through an imbalance and separation between the logical mind of man and his loving heart. Can ones will be free if held in contempt, can ones free expression be boundless if held in contempt, and can ones spirit evolve if held in contempt? For contempt is the off-spring of Judgement and a means of imposing ones will on another. For when the will is not free to co-create, it will then be forced to recreate. Therefore, it is ones fear and ignorance which gives power to re-creation and it is ones love and service which gives power to co-creation. Overcome fear and ignorance, transform and overcome this world of judgement by accepting your feminine and emotional feeling heart.

T.S. July 29, 2009

Prayer Wheel Flow
On
True Healing

For the past serves the future and is revealed in the present. When we speak of healing in the past sense we are speaking of mending a part of ourselves. When we speak of healing in the future sense we are speaking of curing, strengthening and improving a part of ourselves. True healing cannot be found in a pill; for true healing is found within the teachings of a journey. Many approach healing from a physical perspective unable to see the emotional and spiritual aspects. For you may heal your physical body which is a wonderful accomplishment, but does this mean that are you completely healed? Will a physical healing last indefinitely or will you create and repeat this same situation due to ignorance and a lack of spiritual knowledge? For you cannot find true healing which will help you evolve spiritually without first learning the lessons of accountability and responsibility. You cannot find true healing which will help you evolve spiritually without first acquiring the necessary knowledge and wisdom to appreciate and realize your true inner self. The healing journey teaches and awakens you to you and the healing journey teaches and awakens you to love. The healing journey teaches and awakens you to the Great Spirit within. From a spiritual perspective; if you were to heal your physical body and did not awaken to your true inner self and the Great Spirit within, then you would not be truly healed. From a spiritual perspective; if you were to heal your physical body and did awaken to your true inner self and the Great Spirit within, then you would be truly healed. The physical body is your earthly vehicle that your spirit resides and expresses itself. If you were to harm this vehicle due to ignorance and a lack of spiritual knowledge; what would be the likelihood of harming yourself again if you did not uncover and understand the cause? To make sense of this would require new spiritual knowledge and an understanding of self, this, in order to develop your ability to guide and direct this earthly vehicle. When we speak of true healing in the present sense we are speaking of a passage between the past and future, and an awakening to a journey through which we can learn the essential lessons of love. Listen to your heart and evolve your spiritual self to better protect your physical vehicle.

Prayer Wheel Flow
On
The Great Law

There is no escaping the great law, for it is woven into every aspect of existence and reality. The great law is visible and yet invisible to the physical eye, and is designed to maintain and sustain balance. This great law is cooperation, assistance, and the action of love. For this great law of life is service. Absolutely everyone and everything serves knowingly or unknowingly and willingly or unwillingly. Service has been misunderstood by the masses who still equate service simply as an act of kindness, a religious attribute, and a universal bartering system to negotiate for the necessities and pleasures of life. A Spirit Souls journey to planet earth evolves, develops, and advances through pain, suffering, and service. Even when a soul gives in and succumbs to the temptations of the ego and its selfish desires, a soul cannot escape its true nature of service. All spiritual natural laws are based on this law of service. For if you cheat or steal from others you cannot escape this law of service, if you kill or harm others you cannot escape this law of service, and if you bring illness and disease upon yourself, you cannot escape this law of service. To love and to serve requires and involves giving and receiving, which requires opposites to attract. This is why learning through experience requires duality to exist, contradiction to exist, and an opponent to exist. Without this knowledge, it is easy to judge that which we do not understand, for it is easy to misinterpret that which we do not recognize. Realize, no matter where you are today in life you are serving others and realize you are also being served by others through action, inaction, ignorance and reaction. For this reason, it is essential to awaken to your true essence of unconditional love, unconditional forgiveness, and unconditional service. For service is the great governing law in life, serving to raise, uplift, and strengthen your eternal soul's infinite journey.

T.S. January 12, 2009

Prayer Wheel Flow
On
Selfish Earthbound Ego

One cannot grow and develop without ego; one cannot evolve without overcoming ego and one cannot graduate from this earthly classroom without first realizing their true inner self. For it is ego that keeps one earthbound; selfishness creates bad karma and a manipulated mind is held captive to the magic of illusion unable to uncover truth. You are here to overcome your earthly self and the karmic lessons which serve to awaken your selfish earthbound ego to the virtues and qualities of your selfless higher self. Look upon your ego as a false self, your ephemeral transitory self, serving to uplift your eternal soul. Ego is like an anchor fastening you to a merry-go-round of earthly experiences. Ego is the cause of karma and karma is the effect which keeps you earthbound and stuck in a revolving door of earthly fate and destiny experiences. Ego is the dark shadow serving to awaken you to embrace the light within. For a caterpillar needs to first shed its skin completely with the intention of transforming into a beautiful butterfly. For you need to first shed your ego completely with the intention of transforming into a beautiful loving spirit. For this is the metamorphic process or course required to end karmic lessons of love. The secret to accomplishing this transformation in as little time as possible rests within your heart, and within your willingness and ability to learn your lessons quickly. This means listening to your heart, being guided by your heart, and trusting in your heart. For your heart knows truth, for your heart knows your spirit evolves through selfless service to others, and this is the simple truth, the secret most have been searching for to overcome their selfish earthbound ego.

T.S. September 08, 2009

Prayer Wheel Flow
On
Seeking Fulfillment

You are a spiritual being having a temporary physical experience. Why does a soul choose to experience this temporary physical world? From a physical perspective we seem to be chasing and in search of happiness, joy, peace, and love. From a spiritual perspective we are seeking to better understand and discern infinite happiness, joy, peace, and love. These expressions and qualities are aspects of our infinite endless light within and of our creator. We will not truly be complete or fulfilled until we come to understand and respect this infinite endless light within. Since this physical world offers only a temporary experience; man fails to understand how these brief physical experiences work as the building blocks and stepping stones toward their spiritual fulfillment. Life is an invisible revolving door of physical experiences and many live with the illusion of having only this one chance at life, and as a result seek instant pleasure and gratification in their pursuit of happiness, joy, peace, and love. The difference between seeking pleasure and seeking fulfillment is the difference between the physical world and the spiritual world. For one is temporary and will not last, while the other is infinite and everlasting. Realize and understand that seeking pleasure is needed and necessary to awaken your lower self to recognize the needs of your higher self. Through serving the needs and desires of the lower self, one pays the price to obtain the necessary knowledge and wisdom required to unearth and discern the spiritual fulfillment of the higher self. This earthly classroom of learning and physical experience requires that duality and contradiction exist to prompt self-reflection. This allows the lower self to better serve the higher self to be served by the higher self. Therefore, do not judge the desires of the lower self; for it ignites and fans the flames of spiritual fulfillment.

T.S. June 15, 2009

Prayer Wheel Flow
On
Self-Accountability

For one needs to account for that which is theirs, for one needs to answer to that which is theirs, and one needs to be liable for that which is theirs. Self-accountability is not about blaming, condemning, or shaming, self-accountability is about evaluating, learning, and accepting self. Self-accountability is about awakening to the cause and about awakening to the creation of your life circumstances to better understand the positive and negative effects present. For without self-accountability how can you advance your Spirit and Soul? Without self-accountability how can you find closure and create a new? The spiritual natural law of cause and effect reveals a consequence, a result, and an effect will follow every act, deed, provocation, motive or cause; for you are implementing this spiritual natural law every second of every minute of every day. Ignorance may serve you well at times, ignorance may be bliss at times, but ignorance, in this case, will only serve to disappoint, frustrate, and desert you. Self-accountability is the great knight in shining armour; the great rescuer of your self-created verdict in life. If you do not awaken to self-accountability you will continue living in your self-created prison of ego, fear, and denial. The most direct route to self-accountability is to accept the simple fact that there are no accidents, coincidences, or things being left to chance in life. Your life has been shaped by the spiritual natural law of cause and effect and you are the cause in your life and your circumstances are the effect. Therefore, do not bury your head in the sand; have courage to face your past, have courage to face your present, and have courage to face your future. Do not fear, but be determined in seeking self-knowledge, do not fear, but be persistent in seeking truth, and do not fear, but persevere with seeking answers to your present life circumstance. The liberating path of self-accountability awaits you.

T.S. December 27, 2008

Prayer Wheel Flow
On
Spiritual Indifference

Life is a spiritual maze of predetermined and prearranged pathways, staircases, mirrors, and obstacles that one has to navigate and overcome by way of determination. Life is a maze of adjustable and changeable pathways, staircases, mirrors, and obstacles that one has to study to gain knowledge and wisdom by way of self-reflection. For many unknowingly choose to journey alone through their spiritual maze, for many are not aware of having an inner guidance system, and thus, many become lost, anxious, and confused by the complexities of life. For everyone has been bestowed with an inner wisdom or spiritual compass to navigate and guide them through life. This spiritual compass allows one to rise above to see below, to awaken to the bird's eye view of the higher self, and to develop a coping attitude of spiritual indifference. The Higher Self knows and understands the predetermined lessons and hidden growth possibilities within one's life on earth, and therefore, is spiritually indifferent to life conditions. Having an attitude of spiritual indifference to cope with life conditions is divine and only a contradiction in its expression. Spiritual indifference means taking responsibility and accountability without surrendering to the clutches or attachments of worry, fear, and despair. Spiritual indifference allows one to have an objective perception as opposed to a subjective perception on life conditions. Spiritual indifference opposes secular indifference; for it is a coping mechanism of the heart while the other is a coping mechanism of the mind. For one serves the Higher Self while the other serves the Lower Self and one serves love while the other serves fear. Spiritual indifference is an attitude; it is objective, unconditional, universal, and it is divine in nature. Spiritual indifference allows you to cope with the present moment with a sense of balance, peace, and a knowing that all will be well. Realize your soul would never intend or design a spiritual maze for your life that you could not navigate through and overcome.

T.S. February 22, 2010

Prayer Wheel Flow
On
Temptation

The dividing line is thin, the dividing line is vague, and the dividing line is vulnerable to ones way of thinking. Religions panel of judges view temptation to be evil having no divine benefit, for religions panel of judges view temptation to be immoral having no divine principle, and religions panel of judges view temptation to be unethical having no divine value. Any view that is judgmental and one-sided is misleading and lacking in divine awareness. If everything created is from an unconditional loving divine creator, then would it be correct to assume everything has unconditional divinity, goodness, and kindness contained within it? For there is no good or bad, no right or wrong; for man cannot live without rain and man cannot live without sun as both serve man equally. Therefore, it is vain and useless to judge rain as bad simply because you would rather feel the warmth of the sun shining upon your face. To learn and understand the value of love, your higher self requires duality and contradiction to exist in a physical world of illusion. For does the dark not have to serve the light to be served by the light. Does illness not have to serve health to be served by health, and does hate not have to serve love to be served by love in a world of duality and contradiction? Therefore, temptation is ignorance serving knowledge in order to be served by knowledge in a world of duality and contradiction. This, to awaken your lower self to recognize and realize the wisdom, knowledge, and guidance of your higher self; for this is your lower self-serving your higher self to be served by your higher self. Temptation serves as a catalyst and as a method of discovering and uncovering the Great Spirit within. You are constantly being tempted and persuaded to discover and uncover the wisdom, knowledge, and guidance of your true higher self; for all is service, for all is love, and all just is.

T.S. April 20, 2009

Prayer Wheel Flow
On
Stay in the Light

What does it mean to stay in the light and where do we find this light? When we speak of a light within we are speaking of a place that is gentle, untroubled, and a place that is full of life. For the physical symbol of Divine, the Great Spirit, Creator, God, Allah, or whichever name you may wish to use is the brilliant, amazing, and impressive sun in the sky. For the sun has tremendous power and is ever so gentle; the sun has blinding brightness and radiates tender warmth, and the sun has been misunderstood and cursed and still serves unconditionally. You have a spark of this brilliant light within you; for it is your soul. Your soul rests within your heart and uses the physical heart to communicate with you. For this is why your heart knows truth; this is why your heart has knowledge and wisdom, and this is where you'll find your conscience and common sensibility. This is also your inner wisdom, guidance, and message center; know that you are never alone in this physical world of illusion. To become aware of this light within is not enough, for you need to develop faith and courage to recognize, trust, and follow the message of your soul within. This is a relationship which you need to cultivate with your heart; for this is a communication which you need to foster with your heart and this is a marriage which you need to nurture with your heart. It is important to stay in this light; you must realize and understand that the darkness will always resist this light. This is your greatest protection, security, and shelter in life. For all darkness; your challenges, obstacles, and difficulties in life need to be balanced within this light of truth which rests within your heart. This will allow you to transform any and all fears into hope and this will allow you to transform any and all fears into love. Recognize your biggest enemy in life is fear and fear originates in the mind and not in the heart. Therefore, live with confidence every day from your heart and not from your mind; for your mind is here to assist your heart and not the other way around.

T.S. March 2, 2009

Prayer Wheel Flow
On
Spiritual Ego

Enlightenment is the eternal path of all souls; enlightenment is also an infinite journey of discovery. For all experiences, good or bad, are a means to nurture and nourish the progression toward higher spiritual enlightenment. For the ego is a friend and a supporter of spiritual enlightenment. The ego is an adversary and an opponent of spiritual enlightenment. Enlightenment is not about the death of the ego; enlightenment is about the transformation of the ego. Enlightenment is another word for understanding, awareness and knowledge. For each individual has his or her own level of enlightenment within a multitude of personality traits that transcends religious and non-religious beliefs. For one needs to be cautious of the ego which says, I am more enlightened than those who are religious, as well as, the ego which says, I am more enlightened than those who are non-religious. Spiritual enlightenment is an individual personal journey which extends beyond classifications or organizations. Absolute and complete enlightenment belongs to the infinite; for it is eternal. All souls are on a path toward enlightenment regardless of their present earthly beliefs. All souls having an earthly experience are living beings in search of infinite knowledge, truth, and wisdom to better understand their true self.

T.S. January 19, 2009

Prayer Wheel Flow
On
Illness is Soul Medicine

Illness is not a life and death circumstance, for death is an illusion and anything that belongs to illusion is not real. The physical body is an illusion; it is impermanent and will disappear in time. Illness being part of the physical body is also an illusion, for it is impermanent and will disappear in time. Life is real and life is everlasting, for you are real and you are everlasting. For life is infinite and therefore you are also infinite, and that which is infinite does not know death. You are infinite knowledge, truth, wisdom, and love. Illness is a lesson of life and not a lesson of death. Illness is an opportunity to awaken to the intangible you, the infinite you, the real you, and illness is an opportunity to awaken to the Great Spirit that rests within you. Illness is self-medication; illness is like a bitter pill, a bitter potion, and a bitter medicine intended to heal and awaken you to truth beyond illusion. For this is the law of cause and effect in action, this is the law of sowing what you reap, and this is the law of reflection. These spiritual self-governing laws are intended to guide and protect you from self-destruction. Imagine being encased, and surrounded by an invisible mirror. Imagine every thought, intention, action or inaction emitting energy. This energy transmits certain vibrations and frequencies of light that reflect off this invisible mirror back to you. What you have caused will be reflected back to you as the effect, and what you have sowed will be reflected back to you as the harvest. This is your invisible mirror of likeness reflecting accountability, responsibility, compensation and liability. For this is what it means to cast your bread upon the waters, for the bread you cast is the bread you will eat. Therefore beware, for the bread you are eating today is the same bread you cast yesterday, and the bread you are casting today will be the bread of tomorrow. So do not blame others for your life circumstances, and do not blame god for your life circumstances, for you are the only true architect of your life; for you are governed by spiritual natural law. Therefore, think twice before you act or react, and think twice before this soul medicine of illness becomes the only remedy left to awaken you to the real you.

Prayer Wheel Flow
On
Experience

Experience has no equal, experience has no substitute and experience has no rival. For what you read cannot equal, substitute or rival an actual physical experience, for what you see cannot equal, substitute or rival an actual physical experience and what you hear cannot equal, substitute or rival an actual physical experience. True learning, knowledge, and wisdom can only be acquired through an actual physical experience. You may read, see, and hear on war, but you will never know or understand war until you have the actual physical experience of war. You may read, see, and hear on illness, but you will never know or understand illness until you have the actual physical experience of illness. Ignorance and fear criticizes and judges that which we do not understand and those who we do not understand. For when we walk a mile in another's shoes, ignorance and fear transforms and evolves into knowledge. This knowledge becomes the substance and essence of wisdom. For the soul learns, evolves, and expands greatest through having physical experiences. Real compassion, appreciation, courage, faith, and love cannot be taught by words alone. Words are not enough to deliver the essence, spirit, soul and real meaning of an actual physical experience. Experience is your parent in this physical world, for it teaches through consequence and it teaches through compensation. Therefore, one should pay attention and learn the lessons of their experiences, for experience is guidance, direction and is a path of enlightenment. For the "why" of your physical experience has many faces depending upon ones perception. To best understand the "why" of one's physical experience look within your heart; for the relationship to the heart is the key to understanding your physical life experiences. Through patience, trust, and time, your path of experiences will be revealed to you as a knowing which exists deep within your heart.

T.S. January 20, 2009

Prayer Wheel Flow
On
Divine Ego

Ones ego is not evil and ones ego is not immoral; for the ego is misunderstood and misinterpreted. For like a child whom doesn't know right from wrong, is easily influenced, is needy and is self-centered; the ego is the child in you that wants to receive. For a child in its formative years learns more about receiving than giving, and this teaches and conditions the developing ego to want and receive more. For your ego responds to your will; if you are feeling happy the ego wants more happiness, and if you are feeling sad the ego wants more sadness. For your ego is protecting what it thinks you want and what it believes is in your best interest. For the ego is as divine as anything else, for it is a divine part of you, and yet, many believe the death of the ego is necessary in order to evolve spiritually. There can be no recognition of oneself without the ego, for it is the ego which gives one a sense of self and protects ones present ability to express oneself. It is ego which allows one to recognize the difference between oneself and everything else. The ego needs to be accepted and not denied in order to evolve. The ego needs to recognize and understand that it too needs to evolve spiritually with you. A healthy ego needs to be balanced within the heart, for it is the heart which brings a sense of balance to every part of your being. The ego becomes problematic when there is an imbalance created by the erroneous mind, for the erroneous mind influenced by illusion will manipulate the ego. For like a child, ones ego needs to be protected and nourished with love. For like a child, ones ego needs to be accepted unconditionally, and like a child, ones ego needs daily guidance, direction, and leadership from ones loving heart.

T.S. December 08, 2008

Prayer Wheel Flow
On
Behind a Veil of Matter

This is a world camouflaged by matter, this is a world suppressed by delusion, and this is a world created through perception. Our eyes cannot see that which gives life to matter; for there is a vibrant energetic world of light, molecules and particles constantly vibrating and dancing all around us. For there is a vibrant energetic world of light, molecules and particles constantly vibrating and dancing within us. For one should question the need to conceal what is real, what is truth, and the logic and wisdom behind creating a world camouflaged by matter. For this is all part of a process and manner of development designed to uncover and discover truth. This is how we expand our soul consciousness for the purpose of co-creation enlightenment. For all truth is in a state of breakthrough to be liberated by way of discernment. All truth is in a state of discovery to be set free by way of experience, and all truth is in a state of reveal to be released through consequence or outcome. Truth has to be desired and sought, and truth has to be learned in order to be respected. Each lesson of truth learned creates a piece to a puzzle; each piece of this puzzle is akin to a single reincarnation in life. The goal is to create and complete your puzzle with the least amount of pieces or reincarnations possible. This unlocks the doors of ascension to experience higher dimensions and levels of truth. This is a lengthy and yet transitory experience, illusionary and yet real experience, intricate but yet a straightforward progression toward graduation from planet earth. Behind a veil of matter lives another world with its own rules and perceptions that extend beyond the boundaries of our three dimensional world. One should not be fooled into thinking that they are separate or detached in any way from having an effect or influence on this world; for you are already an intricate and creative partner of this world.

T.S. January 25, 2010

Prayer Wheel Flow
On
Awakening Thy True Self

When the student is ready, thy true divine self will begin to appear. Once the student is in a position to purify and cleanse their heart, their real identity will gradually become known to them. There are no accidents to awaken one to their true divine self; for all experiences, events, and happenings answer to spiritual natural law. When the moment or time of self-development is right, the proper conditions will appear to raise the consciousness further. Man dwells within a system of self-development through which self-identification is at the core of each experience. Each experience creates further complementary or balancing experiences of advancement to awaken the outer self to recognize the inner self. To awaken to thy true divine self one has to first become lost. To awaken to thy true divine self, one has to first be placed into darkness, and to awaken to thy true divine self, one has to first learn to overcome challenges. The true self needs to understand itself before it can truly evolve. To have been given everything without knowledge and understanding can only leave thy true self unfulfilled and in a state of wanting more. For this is a world of reflection and through a physical experience the temporary self is inspired and encouraged to question, discern, and discover its true eternal self. By taking on a different form, a temporary physical form, the soul's consciousness is provided with a means of reflection to understand its spiritual identity. A life experience does not define you, but rather awakens you to find the real you.

Prayer Wheel Flow
On
Acceptance

For what is the true nature and spirit of acceptance and what is the heartfelt essence of acceptance? For the path of acceptance has been plagued with hypocrisy. The expression of acceptance has been overflowing with egotism and the appearance of acceptance has been masked by a veil of artificiality. For the true nature of acceptance is not about tolerating others; the real spirit of acceptance is not about feeling pity for others, and the heartfelt essence of acceptance is not about trying to physically co-exist. For these are the inconsistent moral teachings taught within religion, and these are the conformist's misguided veils of judgment. True acceptance is unconditional in nature and pure in spirit. Heartfelt acceptance is self-appreciation, self-realization, and self-love in essence. To truly value and accept others unconditionally one must first value and accept oneself unconditionally. To truly value and accept others unconditionally one must understand that sin is not a sin; for there is no such thing as a sinner. To truly value and accept others unconditionally one needs to understand and realize the evolutionary nature of their soul. The Great Spirit of Divine would never create a sinner; for you are a soul part of the Great Spirit and your true essence can only be love. For the Great Spirit created your earthly classmates and your earthly soul mates with the same true essence of love. Your spiritual journey is the same as your earthly soul mates; for you are all here to experience this physical life to further evolve and expand your knowledge and wisdom of love. Therefore, true acceptance is beyond right or wrong, true acceptance is beyond good or bad and true acceptance is beyond you or me; for true acceptance understands and appreciates that all is one, all is just, and all just is.

T.S. January 03, 2009

Prayer Wheel Flow
On
Lifting Your Service

The ego seeks to serve itself while the purpose of the inner self is to serve others. Genuine truth is realized and becomes conscious through the intention and the ability of the inner self to serve others. Falsehood and hypocrisy is the consequence and by-product of the ego turning inward to serve itself. This is how a soul comes to be lost in a world of duality. Yet, this is a necessary and essential step on the path to discovering and uncovering your true inner self. These steps speak to the many lifetimes on the staircase toward truth; truth is love and love is service. The ego creates the need and hunger for truth, love, and service within a world of duality. The conscience of the soul, through the use of forgiveness, creates the balance needed to move forward. This wisdom of balance is maintained and secured by taking responsibility and being accountable for one's past. Without forgiveness the self cannot find closure to then create a new. Finding closure to create a new awakens the inner self to the outer self; this is always done with the assistance of others. Helping others lift their service is how one lifts their own service. To advance and progress beyond the experiences of earth through service is a means to an end. However, life on earth represents but a fraction of the eternal ring of service; for the lessons of love and service are endless. Therefore, the message received, "I want to lift your service" supports eternal oneness and expresses unconditional love that is present and exists within the self.

T.S. June 21, 2011

Prayer Wheel Flow
On
Guidance for Difficult Times

The birth of a new day is all you have; for you do not know what is to come. You must decide how you will live this day. It is your freewill choice that decides what path to take. To open your eyes is not to be fully awake; for your eyes alone cannot guide you. Being from the spirit realm, you must awaken to your heart. Your heart is your guide and your mind is its assistant. You must awaken your mind daily to recognize your heart. Your mind is like a child, it needs daily guidance from you. Your mind has magnificent potential to create and you must not allow your mind to roam wild; for it does not know truth. For when I say "you" I mean the spirit within. It is your responsibility to bring awareness to the mind. For you are here to assist the soul, therefore listen to the soul and do not be tempted by illusion. It is through the heart that you will find guidance. Your heart connects you to your spirit guide and to the voice of your soul. This is where the light of truth and wisdom awaits your calling to serve you. Your words, thoughts, and intentions will enable you to connect to this light within and bridge the mind and heart daily. In this way you receive guidance daily and also awaken fully to your journey. Ground your energy daily with this mantra for light and love; for this is your true essence. This mantra must be recited slowly:

Stay In the Light

Today I Choose to See the Light
Today I Choose to Receive the Light
Today I Choose to Feel the Light
Today I Choose to Be the Light
Today I Choose to Trust the Light
Today I Choose to Follow the Light
Today I Choose to Give the Light
Today I Choose to Be the Real Me

Prayer Wheel Flow
On
Abundant Well-Being

In a world of duality abundant well-being for all is not realized unless there is balance or oneness. Achieving balance and oneness is required to understand love. To understand love is to know truth; there is only one truth and that is love. Truth and love form the heart of man; and balance and oneness live in the heart of man. Within the heart of man exists wisdom and within this wisdom there is oneness, equality, compassion, and service. We evolve and progress by way of this knowledge and life experiences help awaken us to this knowledge. We evolve and progress by way of our true essence of unconditional love and forgiveness. For in a world of duality, man needs to attain a level of knowledge that is spiritual in nature to order to attain this balance and truth. For this is how the doors of real and lasting abundance will open for all. For real possibilities of a world with abundant well-being abound for those who act from their heart with love and compassion. For real possibilities of a world with abundant wellbeing deteriorates for those who act from their mind with greed and contempt. For man must come together and unite their intellectual mind and feeling heart to better serve one another. Service cultivates true abundance for all without the need for scarcity, famine, poverty or suffering to exist. Real abundance cannot be experienced within a division or condition of duality. For when you have a division or condition of duality, you have opposing views and you have fear and disharmony. There will always be winners and losers, right and wrong, rich and poor, strong and weak, smart and foolish, success and failure. For when you have balance or a condition of oneness, you have love and compassion, and you have a world governed by truth and wisdom to offer abundant well-being for all.

T.S. January 11, 2010

Prayer Wheel Flow
On
An Eye for an Eye

Many followers of truth are near-sighted and many followers of truth are far-sighted; for many lack perfect vision. What is the true meaning and significance behind the quote "an eye for an eye?" Many believe this quote represents self-respect, self-worth, and dignity thereby suggesting one should stand their ground and not allow others to take advantage of them. For contained within this theory exists an undercurrent which suggests a justification and rationalization for retribution and so-called justice. Complete and absolute truth is infinite, endless, and everlasting; for it does not change. You can alter and manipulate truth through ignorance and by way of desire. A misinterpretation of truth creates an illusion which leads to delusion. The true meaning of "an eye for an eye" is to do with accountability and taking personal responsibility in order to maintain and sustain harmony and balance within this physical world of matter. For "an eye for an eye" is a spiritual natural law of self-reflection; your mirror image of accountability which will manifest a like image and visual portrait of your actions. This is to say, if you harm others you in turn harm yourself, "an eye for an eye." If you judge others, you in turn judge yourself, "an eye for an eye." If you serve others, you in turn serve yourself, "an eye for an eye." This is spiritual law that serves to maintain balance and also serves to support a consideration law which states, "Do onto others as you would have others do onto you."

T.S. February 1, 2009

Prayer Wheel Flow
On
Proper Use of Will

To accomplish any mission of truth requires the proper use of Will. To accomplish any mission of truth requires the proper use of determination, mind, desire, and want. For the spirit within needs to be involved and engaged to overcome self and life's untruth. The proper use of Will arises from the spirits persistent determination and resolve to create and discern. For this is an inherent natural ability that can only serve truth if connected to and guided by unconditional love. Unconditional love cannot exist without courage, for this unity produces and is the cause of real faith. Therefore, courage and faith are essential to overcome life's fear and untruth. The proper use of Will accepts and believes only in the power of good. For this power of good is dependable and knows no boundaries, this power of good bestows a compassionate light of peace. Thy Wills have been imprisoned and thy Wills are not truly free. A mission of truth is a mission to liberate and free Wills. Therefore, one should say I will follow truth, I will have courage, I will believe and trust in the power of good and in the power of love, and I will have unwavering faith for this is the proper use of Will.

Prayer Wheel Flow
On
Magical World of Illusion

We live in a magical world of physical matter; for we live in a magical world of fantasy, desire, and illusion. This magical world of illusion is ones earthly classroom of discovery to uncover reality, truth, and the Great Spirit within. For all light casts forth a dark shadow and all shadows belong to the light. It is the dark shadow that teaches one to develop a compassionate heart and strengthen ones eternal soul to see the light of truth within. This serves to ready ones soul for its eternal journey beyond this world of matter. Like a seed that gets planted into the dark ground needing nourishment in order to rise up and serve in the light; you are like a seed planted into this magical world of illusion in search of your true light. This magical world of illusion is only but one of the infinite evolutionary spiritual classrooms designed to strengthen and enlighten ones eternal soul. Many are misled and get caught up in chasing the illusion, the shadow, the impermanent, and as a result become earthbound and trapped within a revolving door of physical life experiences, unable to see beyond the shadow of life. For a magician is the Master of illusion, distraction, and the Master of diversion. Though truth is in plain view, one is unable to see this truth; for what is real becomes invisible and what is not real becomes visible. One must question what the reasoning mind wants to reject to recognize this magic of illusion. For one must seek what the reasoning mind wants to reject to discover this magic of illusion, and one must not fear what the reasoning mind wants to reject to study this magic of illusion. Illusion is temporary and all that belongs to illusion is not real and will vanish in time. Man praises, admires, and honours those who accumulate temporary material riches. For who are the wise, those who accumulate temporary material riches or those who accumulate eternal riches of the soul that are infinite? For we are souls partaking in a physical human experience, yet our eyes of matter are unable to see this truth. This magic of illusion is revealed for all to see when the physical body fails, but yet again, man fails to question what his reasoning mind wants to reject. For the eternal soul is real and yet invisible to the physical eyes of matter, and the temporary physical body is not real and yet visible to the eyes of matter; a perfect magical illusion. Only the magical light of truth will free one from this magical spell of illusion. For this magical light of truth within flows through the heart and is compassion, gratitude, kindness, thoughtfulness, and this magical light of truth within is unconditional forgiveness, unconditional love, and unconditional service.

T.S. Aug 6, 2008

Prayer Wheel Flow On Sin is Not a Sin

Only the light of truth will remove the darkness of sin, for the true meaning of sin shall be revealed in the light. The Great Spirit of Love is perfect and all that is created is also perfect. Birth is as perfect as death; a short physical life experience is as perfect as a long physical life experience. The natural laws that govern life are perfect; all life lessons are perfect, and the imperfect use of freewill is also perfect. Life is infinite and all that belongs to life is also infinite, including knowledge, wisdom, truth, and love. The learning never ends; mistakes are perfect stepping stones on the path toward infinite knowledge, infinite wisdom, infinite truth, and infinite love. This is how god created man to evolve in this physical world, and therefore how can man create sins against his creator? How can man be defined by his actions and be called a sinner? If the Great Divine intended man to be all-knowing, than the purpose and path of enlightenment would not exist, and therefore man would not exist. Man must first graduate from the lessons of planet earth to move up to the next level of love of a higher frequency; for these dimensions of love are infinite and endless beyond human imagination. The Great Divine did not create a single sinner, this is but a creation from the mind of man, and this is a school of thought taught by theologians with its roots founded upon fear. Sin is a subjective word used by man to describe what is believed to be morally wrong. What is considered bad to one group may not be to another; all experiences are part of a natural progression toward higher knowledge, higher wisdom, and higher truth. Your true spiritual nature and your true self can never be defined by a mistake, but you will be held responsible and accountable to your mistakes by the natural universal law of cause and effect. You are your only true salvation in life, work with this natural law and reap a sweet harvest, work contrary to this law and reap a bitter harvest. This is not the wrath of God; this is not a punishment from God. You are bound by the natural laws that govern life. Learn to work with these laws and not oppose them. God is love and love does not punish, love does not judge, love does not condemn; true love serves with compassion. Have no fear for you are not a sinner, become one with your heart; trust in your heart for you are a spirit created from love, a perfect spark of Divine Love.

T.S. June 20, 2008

Unlock Your Spiritual Self
To
Know Who You Are....

Set Yourself Free

31110512R00070

Made in the USA
Charleston, SC
06 July 2014